BURPEE®

Burpee Basics

roses

A growing guide for easy, colorful gardens

Mary C. Weaver

Macmillan • USA

MACMILLAN
A Simon & Schuster Macmillan Company
1633 Broadway
New York, NY 10019

MACMILLAN is a registered trademark of Macmillan, Inc.

BURPEE is a registered trademark of W. Atlee Burpee & Company

Library of Congress Cataloging-in-Publication Data

Weaver, Mary C.
    Roses : a growing guide for easy, colorful gardens / by Mary C. Weaver.
        p.   cm. — (Burpee basics)
    Includes bibliographical references and index.
    ISBN 0-02-862636-2 (alk. paper)
    1. Rose culture.   2. Roses—Varieties.   I. Title.   II. Series.
SB411.W4 1998   98-30533
635.9'33734—dc21   CIP

Manufactured in the United States of America

10 9 8 7 6 5 4 3 2 1

Book design by Nick Anderson
Cover design by Michael Freeland
Cover photograph courtesy W. Atlee Burpee
Photography credits:
    All America Rose Selections: ii, 69(bottom), 71
    Peter Haring: 9, 32, 43, 46, 48, 49(top), 50(bottom), 51, 54, 55, 57, 58, 59(bottom), 60(top),
        61, 62(top), 64, 65(top), 67(bottom), 68, 70(top), 74, 75, 76(top), 78, 82, 83(top), 84(top),
        86(bottom), 87, 88 (top) 89, 91, 92, 96, 98, 99(bottom), 102
    Mike Lowe: xvi, 14, 45, 47(top), 52, 59(top), 60(bottom), 62(bottom), 77, 83(bottom),
        84(bottom), 90, 93, 100
    Greg Piotrowski: 7, 9(left), 29, 47(bottom), 49(bottom), 50(top), 65(bottom), 66, 67(top),
        69(top), 70(bottom), 76(bottom), 81, 85, 86(top), 88(bottom), 97, 99(top), 112, 124, 129,
        132, 137(top), 139(bottom), 140, 143(top), 144
    Baldo Villegas: 130, 131, 137(bottom), 139(top), 141, 142, 143(bottom)
Line drawings by Laura Robbins

This book is dedicated to my wonderful parents, Noella and Harold Peterson, who taught me to strive for worthy goals and always to do my best; to dear friends and associates Marie Hofer and Becky Menn-Hamblin, who saw this idea germinate and helped it grow; and especially to my husband, Steve Weaver, whose unwavering love and support made it possible.

Burpee Basics: Growing Guides for Easy, Colorful Gardens
Down-to-earth handbooks for beginning gardeners

Available from Macmillan Publishing

Burpee Basics: Annuals, by Emma Sweeney
Burpee Basics: Perennials, by Emma Sweeney
Burpee Basics: Roses, by Mary C. Weaver
Burpee Basics: Bulbs, by Douglas Green

To order a Burpee catalogue:

order toll-free 1-800-888-1447
www.burpee.com

or write:

W. Atlee Burpee & Co.
300 Park Avenue
Warminster, PA 18974

Contents

Foreword

Gardeners have been looking to Burpee for basic information about how to garden, as well as the seeds and plants to implement their dreams, for almost 125 years. In one or the other of the six different catalogs we publish each year, a gardener can find just about any kind of plant his or her heart desires. Our big annual seed catalogue, the *Burpee Annual*, has become a gardening bible. (If you've never had the pleasure of paging through one, there's information on page vi about how to get your own free copy.)

What you hold in your hands—one of our new series of concise gardening guidebooks—is a continuation of that proud tradition of giving gardeners the essentials they need. These handy little books have a great deal in common with seeds: each one contains all you need to start a wonderful gardening experience, one that will grow year by year. Successful gardens are built upon a constant reworking of the fundamentals. Even the most experienced gardeners, season after season, attend to the basic practices that you'll find so skillfully explained in these guides.

If you're a novice gardener, *Burpee Basics* will help you to find quickly the information you need to get started; those of you who are more seasoned can use the books as invaluable reference tools to remind yourself when to start the marigold seeds or divide the anemones, how to cut back the roses or determine the right amount of fertilizer for daffodils . . . all the details you need to keep your plants at their best.

We've made these books a convenient size as well as easy on the eyes, hoping they'll find a valued spot, not on your coffee table but on the shelf above your potting bench or in your garden workroom, right next to your seed packets, where they'll become as well-worn and comfortable in your hand as a favorite trowel or trusty clippers.

George Ball, Jr.

Acknowledgments

To those who generously provided information and expertise, many thanks: Phyllis Allen, Christin Anderson, Phil Ash, Frank Baier, Frances Ballentine, Gail and Roger Barnett, Adra Benton, Dave Berg, Earl and Leola Bott, Russ Bowermaster, Lilyan and Martin Brower, David Byrne, Jackie Clark, Susan Clingenpeel, Louise Coleman, Doug Dalton, Barbara Daly, Joyce Dillon, Liz Druitt, Phil Edmunds, Aaryn Flick, Steve Gavey, Sarah Sue Goldsmith, Steve Graf, Deborah Green, Heather Hallworth, Patty Hance, Peter Haring, Gordon Holcomb, Steve Hutton, Jeri Jennings, Bud Jones, Steve Jones, Sam Kedem, Nancy Lewis, Bruce Lind, Nancy Lindley, Marlynn Marcks, Sam McGredy, Teresa Milligan, Pat Mitchell, Collette Morton, Tom and Lois Mui, Bill Nettles, Pam Palmer, John Parks, Mary Peterson, Tim Raiford, Lindi Reagan, Nancy Redington, Sonia Richardson, Diane Ridout, Susan Saxton, Phillip Schorr, Diane Schrift, Donna Smoot, Barbara Stauch, Cynthia Sutton, Debra Teachout-Teashon, Patty Thigpen, Lynn Thomson, Patti Tobin, Marlon Villa, Baldo Villegas, Charles Walker, Cathy Walworth, Bert Wheeler, Mark Whitelaw, Ann Wickenhauser, and Mark Wiederin.

To my agent, Richard Parks, who believed in this project and in me, my deepest gratitude. I am also indebted to this book's editor, Barbara Berger, for her thorough and professional assistance, technical reader Greg Piotrowski, who has an eagle eye and knows roses inside and out, and production editor Arun Das, for his careful attention to every detail of the production process.

Introduction

You're interested in growing roses or you wouldn't have picked up this book. Who wouldn't be? Roses are the epitome of romance and beauty—the loveliest and often the most deliciously scented flowers around. They come in an amazing range of colors, shapes, and sizes, from tiny miniatures to thirty-foot climbers, from simple wild roses to sensuous, petal-packed heirloom varieties and modern high-centered hybrid teas.

But if you haven't grown roses—or if you've had bad experiences with them—you may believe they're more trouble than they're worth. That roses are strictly for experts.

Bosh. There's no magic, no mystery to rose gardening. You can succeed at it, whether you're an absolute novice or a veteran gardener. It's a matter of understanding and offering what roses need: good soil, plenty of sunshine, water and fertilizer, pruning, and protection from disease and insects. None of these tasks are beyond the beginning gardener, and this book will give you clear, step-by-step instructions and the confidence you need to create and maintain a beautiful rose garden.

Part 1 explains the importance of choosing robust plants and proper planting sites so that you can begin with high-quality roses and put them in the right places. Part 2 presents everything you need to know about preparing rich soil so your roses will thrive. In part 3 you'll learn about the different classes of roses and find descriptions and, in most cases, photographs of

100 beautiful and healthy cultivars, old and new. Part 4 outlines ordinary care for roses, offering easy-to-follow guidelines for watering, fertilizing, pruning, and providing winter protection, as needed. Part 5 discusses the diseases and insects that may plague roses, giving you prevention strategies and recommending both nontoxic and conventional methods of control. At the end of the book you'll find lists of resources to help you learn more about the queen of flowers.

Don't be afraid to give roses a try. Sure, they take a little more time than azaleas or irises. But once you invite these intoxicating beauties into your garden, you won't want to live without them.

Mary C. Weaver

giving any rose a good start

The Essentials

- Selection: Choosing Good Plants
- Site: Assessing Your Garden

It's nearly impossible for rose lovers to look at pictures of gorgeous gardens and not want to rush out, buy plants, and start sticking them in the ground. But please read this part and part 3, "The Rose Gallery," before you choose plants, then read part 2, "Doing the Spadework," before you start digging.

Why this tiresome delay? Rose gardening is one of those endeavors in which your chance of success depends almost wholly on whether you start out well or badly. Much of the really important work—selecting healthy, disease-resistant plants, choosing the right site, and preparing good soil— takes place at the beginning. Think of it as prenatal care for your embryonic rose garden.

If you take note of the three S's—selection, site, and soil—you'll have laid the foundation for a vigorous rose garden and greatly minimized your future troubles. Naturally, your garden's ongoing performance also depends on the weather and ordinary seasonal and day-to-day care, but no amount of reme-dial work can make up for faulty choices or preparation on the front end. In other words, if you put low-quality, disease-prone plants in a wonderful site or top-notch roses in a poor site, there's not much you can do later to over-come it except replace or move the plants.

What you learn in this part and the next will help you lay the foundation for a robust and satisfying rose garden that will provide years of pleasure.

Selection: Choosing Good Plants

What's a good plant? Certainly it should be healthy to begin with, and if you want to make your life easier and improve the odds in your favor, it should be at least moderately disease-resistant (see part 3). That sounds simple enough—yet beginning rose gardeners are bombarded with unfamiliar terms from the start. As you shop, you'll learn that you can't simply buy a rose— you must choose bare-root or containerized plants; own-root or grafted; grade 1, $1^1/_2$, or 2; and from mail-order catalogs or local garden centers. Here's a rundown on those terms as well as tips on deciding which options are right for you and your garden.

Bare-root or Containerized

A bare-root rose is simply a dormant plant that is shipped to the consumer or a nursery with no soil around its roots. Bare-root plants are grown in fields (mainly in California and Arizona), harvested when nearly dormant, stripped of leaves, and kept in temperature-controlled cold storage at about 33°F until spring planting time. Although bare-root roses may look downright dead, they readily spring into life within a few weeks of planting. If you look carefully, you should be able to see pinkish swellings on the canes (the horticultural term for a rose's main stems): those are the bud eyes, nodes from which new canes, leaves, and finally flowers will appear.

Bare-root roses are usually shipped with moist wood shavings or excelsior around their roots and encased in heavy plastic. A healthy plant should have a well-developed, well-proportioned root system and green, full-looking canes with creamy white pith (the softer tissue within the stem). You should see no signs of fungus or irregular swellings on roots or top growth, and none of the canes should be shriveled or discolored. If a plant doesn't meet those standards, ask the vendor to replace it. Bare-root roses should be kept moist and cool (35 to 40°F) and in their packages until they can be planted. If they must be held for longer than two weeks, dig a trench in the garden, remove the roses' packaging, place them in the trench at a 45-degree angle, and cover them with soil until you're able to plant them properly.

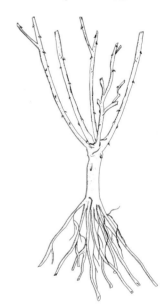

A healthy bare-root rose has a well-balanced, well-developed root system and firm green canes with white pith.

Containerized plants are sold in pots, although they too are field-grown in most cases. They can be shipped and planted throughout the growing season, whereas bare-root plants can be shipped only in early spring, while they're dormant.

Which is better? It's really a matter of personal preference. Both kinds are easy to plant, so don't shy away from bare-root roses on that account. Be aware, though, that if you live in a cool climate where soil is too cold and wet to be worked in early spring, planting sites for bare-root roses should be prepared beforehand, in fall.

Major mail-order nurseries tend to offer bare-root plants because they're lighter and cheaper to ship. Smaller mail-order nurseries and local garden centers typically offer containerized plants. They usually cost a little more because you're paying for the labor and materials involved in potting them.

Own-root or Grafted

All roses used to be reproduced by vegetative propagation: someone takes a softwood cutting (a firm but not woody section from the current season's growth) from a rose, puts the cutting in moist soil or sand, and waits for roots to develop. Each new plant is a genetic clone of its parent.

Home gardeners have been multiplying roses in this fashion since there have been roses in gardens. Indeed, immigrants to the New World brought cuttings of their favorite varieties with them so their gardens would have a touch of home.

Nearly all miniature roses are grown from cuttings, as are some modern shrubs, and a number of smaller rose nurseries routinely propagate all sorts of roses this way. The resulting plants are said to be "growing on their own roots" or called "own-root" roses to distinguish them from grafted plants.

When roses are grafted, two distinct plants are joined together—a tough, vigorous rose that will supply the roots (the rootstock, or understock) and a bud eye from a cultivar (cultivated variety, or commercially introduced plant), which will produce the desired flowers and the plant you see from the ground up.

Large mail-order companies and nurseries that supply garden centers sell predominantly grafted roses because it is much faster and cheaper to produce plants of marketable age and size through grafting than propagating from cuttings. Furthermore, some roses don't readily root or aren't particularly vigorous when growing on their own roots.

Grafting has benefits for the consumer as well, making it possible for nurseries to offer new varieties at affordable prices. New daylily introductions, for example, may cost fifty to one hundred dollars or more because the stock is limited and takes years to build up through the process of dividing established plants. In the case of roses, though, a little bud wood (section of cane from which bud eyes are taken) goes a long way, and nurseries can quickly produce large numbers of plants, keeping costs down.

Some rose lovers have strong preferences one way or the other. One advantage of grafted roses is their greater rate of growth in the garden—a top-quality grafted plant will usually reach its mature size by the second growing season. Own-root plants tend to start out smaller, depending on the company that produced them, and may never attain the size of their grafted cousins.

But own-root plants have some distinct pluses as well. In cold climates, where exposed canes may be killed down to ground level in winter, own-root roses will throw up new canes in spring, presuming the plants are hardy in that zone (see the USDA Plant Hardiness Zone Map on page 160). If a grafted rose is killed to the ground, however, the new canes will likely be those of the rootstock, not the bud wood. That's why some roses mysteriously seem to change identities between seasons, producing the slender canes and unfamiliar flowers of the rootstock, which might be a species, or "wild," rose or a named variety. Commonly used rootstocks include the species multiflora rose (*Rosa multiflora*) and dog rose (*R. canina*) as well as named varieties such as 'Dr. Huey' and 'Manetti'.

Own-root roses also eliminate the problems caused by suckering, that is, the growth of new shoots from the rootstock. Obviously, the identity of any suckers that emerge from an own-root rose is clear. But those that come from below ground on a grafted rose are most likely shoots from the understock and must be removed. (For more information, see the pruning section in part 4.)

Finally, a disease called rose mosaic may appear if a virus-infected cultivar has been budded to a healthy rootstock or vice versa. Unfortunately, it's not uncommon in grafted plants. Mosaic can infect own-root roses too but only if the parent plant was infected. The disease doesn't kill the rose, but it does diminish its garden performance. Before you buy roses, ask the seller whether steps have been taken to ensure the plants are virus-free—and whether they'll be replaced at no charge if the virus appears.

Grades of Roses

Grafted roses are sold as grade 1, grade 1$^1/_2$, or grade 2 plants; own-root roses are not graded, so the size of plants you get from different nurseries may vary greatly.

A grade 1 rose must be two years old when harvested from the field and must have at least three large, healthy canes. Grade 1 roses cost more—typically retailing for nine to sixteen dollars or more per plant—but they're worth it because they're sturdier, more vigorous plants, poised to take off in the garden in their first season. Grade 1$^1/_2$ roses must have two strong canes, and if all goes well, they should eventually catch up with grade 1 plants. Don't bother with grade 2 plants: these ultra-cheap varieties are smaller, often substandard roses that may never grow into good-quality plants.

If your budget is limited, it's better to buy one or two grade 1 roses each season than a half-dozen inferior plants that are likely to disappoint you.

Where to Buy

Shop from a reputable local nursery or established mail-order company (see the appendix for a list of vendors). Beware of those whose prices seem too good to be true, and take note of each merchant's guarantees. Most reputable companies will refund your money if a rose fails during its first growing season.

If you're buying from a local nursery, choose plants with large, green, healthy-looking canes. Avoid plants whose canes look dried out or brownish or whose leaves appear diseased or insect-infested. Most garden centers sell containerized roses, including roses in biodegradable boxes that can be planted.

If a local discount store offers inexpensive bare-root plants packaged in skinny plastic bags, find out when the plants were shipped from the supplier. You don't want to buy roses that have been sitting around unpotted at room temperature for weeks. Another drawback is that these plants' roots must be severely pruned in order to fit them into those small packages. That means they'll start life in your garden at a significant disadvantage. If you prefer bare-root roses, it's better to order them by mail from a reputable nursery. That way you'll get larger plants and can be sure that they've been held in cold storage until shipment.

Certainly it's faster and more convenient to buy from local nurseries, presuming they have what you want, and in a good garden center you'll find salespeople who can answer your questions. You also get the chance to eyeball the merchandise yourself and choose the most robust plants.

On the other hand, the average garden center can stock only a few of the thousands of rose cultivars available in commerce—typically some of the season's new introductions, classics such as hybrid teas 'Peace' and 'Mister Lincoln', perhaps a few of David Austin's popular English roses, and a smattering of modern shrubs. Very few carry many old garden roses, those whose classes were created before 1867.

Fortunately, dozens of mail-order companies in the United States and Canada offer a wide range of roses to suit every taste. A number of catalogs—particularly those of larger companies—are free; others cost a few dollars. All of those mentioned in the appendix are well worth having, and many include

One of the best ways to assess new roses without buying them is to visit a trial or display garden. The Peggy Rockefeller Rose Garden at the New York Botanical Garden is one of more than 130 public gardens accredited by All-America Rose Selections. All feature recent AARS award–winning varieties.

Dozens of new roses are introduced every spring. A few may prove timeless; the others will fade from view in five, ten, or twenty years. One way to sort the sheep from the goats is to pay attention to those honored as All-America Rose Selections (AARS)—hybrid teas, grandifloras, floribundas, miniatures, and landscape shrubs that have been tested in about two dozen trial gardens throughout the United States and have performed well overall.

Of course, the AARS designation is no guarantee that a given plant will succeed in your yard or, for that matter, that you'll like the way it looks, smells, and otherwise performs. But it's a pretty good indication that the rose in question has some desirable qualities.

A nonprofit organization formed in 1938, AARS Inc. sends new roses to public and private gardens throughout the United States and asks their curators to give them ordinary care (water, fertilizer, protection from disease, etc.) and to rank them twice each growing season for two years running. Plants are judged on color, fragrance, vigor, novelty, the form of buds and flowers, foliage, disease resistance, repeat bloom, and other characteristics, and those that perform in an exemplary fashion in most gardens have a chance to be selected AARS winners.

More than 160 plants have received the AARS designation since 1940, the first year the award was given. Past winners include such stars as 'Peace' (1946), 'Queen Elizabeth' (1955), 'Mister Lincoln' (1965), and 'Double Delight' (1977), as well as some that have faded from the scene: 'Forty-niner' (1949), 'Lilibet' (1954), and 'Fusilier' (1958), to name a few. Each year's winners are marked with a distinctive metal tag and are widely available in garden centers and catalogs that carry modern roses.

The AARS designation is only one of the prizes a rose can win, although in the United States it's the most publicized. The American Rose Society (ARS) confers an Award of Excellence for miniature roses, American Rose Center Trial Ground Gold, Silver, and Bronze Certificates, and other honors. Organizations in Germany, France, Ireland, Italy, Scotland, Spain, and other countries award gold medals to promising cultivars. And the World's Favorite Rose is named at the triennial meeting of the World Federation of Rose Societies. This honor's most recent winner was the large-flowered climber 'New Dawn'; previous winners are hybrid teas 'Peace', 'Fragrant Cloud', 'Double Delight', 'Papa Meilland', 'Pascali', and 'Just Joey'; grandiflora 'Queen Elizabeth'; and floribunda 'Iceberg'.

One of the most difficult contests to win is the Anerkannte Deutsche Rose (ADR) trials held in Germany. In order to pass this grueling three-year endurance test, roses must thrive without the application of antifungal or insecticidal sprays. Winners are disease-resistant and also quite hardy. Past honorees include the well-publicized shrub 'Flower Carpet', the hybrid tea 'Elina', the climber 'Compassion', and the miniature rose 'Starina'.

Then there's the ARS's James Alexander Gamble Rose Fragrance Award, bestowed on 'Double Delight', 'Fragrant Cloud', and other varieties that produce delicious perfume. England's equivalent is the Edland Fragrance Medal, whose recipients include 'Fragrant Delight' and 'Pristine'. Interestingly enough, roses with strong fragrance in England aren't always highly scented here.

In the end, your preferences are what determine the winners in your own garden. But it can't hurt to note which varieties the experts find most promising.

Award-winning hybrid tea 'Double Delight' (left) and floribunda 'Iceberg' (right) are among the world's most popular rose varieties.

a wealth of information about roses and their cultivation. It's wise to order as early as possible, ideally in December or January for spring planting, in order to get the plants you want, especially if the company is small and has a limited inventory.

Site: Assessing Your Garden

As you may know, the genus *Rosa* is prone to certain fungal diseases, discussed at length in part 5. And even disease-resistant roses will succumb if they're planted in sites that encourage the development of fungal infections, as a person with a strong constitution will eventually be weakened by poor health habits.

The good news is that the site, or environment, you provide can play a major role in helping to thwart those diseases. The rest of this section and the site-planning checklist on page 12 will help you locate the best spots to plant roses.

Aspect

Roses love sun—preferably six hours or more a day. Ample sunlight, especially morning rays that dry the dew or rain on foliage, helps discourage blackspot, a bothersome fungal disease that can develop only when leaves are wet for at least seven hours. Some roses—for example, hybrid musks, hybrid rugosas, and albas—are more tolerant of shade, but less sun typically means fewer flowers. If you live in a very hot climate, your roses will appreciate some afternoon shade.

If you're not sure whether an otherwise promising spot offers adequate sun for roses, give it a try. If the plants are bedeviled by disease, flower sparsely, and look less than vigorous, dig them up that fall or early the following spring, and move them elsewhere. But perhaps they'll thrive. The plants' performance is the ultimate answer.

Air Circulation

Fungal diseases are generally encouraged by humidity and/or moisture, and good air movement helps speed the evaporation of water on leaves and dissipate still, humid air. Close quarters and restricted air flow, however, encourage the dispersal of spores from one infected plant to its near neighbors. For these reasons roses planted too close to buildings, fences, and each other are more disease-prone than those that have room to breathe.

There's another reason not to crowd roses: when it comes time for weeding and pruning, you'll be glad you have enough room to maneuver around each bush. If you don't, you'll rue the day you planted them as you crawl between fence and rosebush, trying to uproot dandelions and being torn by prickles.

Before planting, consider the rose's mature spread, and bear in mind that in warm climates with long growing seasons roses usually grow much larger. In Northern states, for example, it's usual to plant hybrid teas 18–24 inches apart; in the South an appropriate distance is 36 inches or more. Many shrub roses have spreading habits, some growing nearly as wide as they are tall—or wider. When in doubt, plant farther apart.

Competition

Roses aren't greedy, but they don't like to share their lunch with trees and other voracious plants. In such a competition roses can't win, so avoid planting them near trees such as maples and beeches, whose invasive surface feeder roots spread far and wide. It's amazing how quickly they can take over a well-watered, fertilized garden bed.

Terrain

There's not a lot you can do about the geography of your yard—short of having it graded or terraced—but at least you can choose the most favorable spot for your roses.

A site that's relatively flat is easiest to garden on. Dips and gullies are often boggy, a condition that most roses—with the notable exception of the swamp rose, the species *Rosa palustris*—cannot tolerate. In winter such a site will also be colder than its surroundings, as cold air pools in low spots. Roses planted there may thus suffer more winter dieback (cane damage due to low temperatures and drying winds).

As you envision each possible site for roses, consider the following:

- How much sun does this site receive during spring and summer? Six hours is desirable; four to five hours is usually the minimum.
- Does it receive morning sun? If you must choose between morning sun and afternoon, morning is preferable. The area east of your house will have morning sun and afternoon shade; the south side will be sunny most of the day.
- Will anything reduce air circulation among roses planted here? Consider buildings, fences, other plantings, and any other barriers. Keeping in mind the roses' mature size, leave at least 1 or 2 feet between them and any barriers.
- If you're planting near a foundation, make sure the roses won't be installed under the roof's drip line.
- Is the site flat or sloping? Avoid slopes and gullies.
- How close are the nearest large trees? The greater the distance, the better.
- How good is the soil in the spots you're considering—and how's the drainage? It will take more work to turn compacted soil into a rose garden. To check the drainage, dig a hole approximately 18 inches deep, and fill it with water. If it takes more than an hour for the water to disappear, you should improve the drainage by aerating the soil and adding sand and organic matter. If heavy-duty soil amendment isn't practical for you, consider planting in a raised bed or in containers.

Steep slopes are usually dry because water runs off rather than soaks in. A few roses—for example, some drought-tolerant species and some hybrids of the species *Rosa rugosa*—could endure a dry slope, but most would find it an extreme challenge. If you must garden on a slope, consider having a portion of it terraced. It will be much easier to keep the soil consistently moist.

Once you've settled on the best possible spot, it's time to get your hands dirty. Part 2, "Doing the Spadework," explains how to prepare soil for planting roses. You might also want to begin flipping through part 3, "The Rose Gallery," and deciding which roses to start with.

doing the spadework

The Essentials

- The Lowdown on Dirt
- Dig It
- Taking Care of Your New Plants: Watering and Mulching

We think of creating a beautiful garden as a creative process—and of course, it is, what with choosing plant shapes and colors that will look good together and designing flower beds and borders. But before the delights of a blooming rose garden comes the thoroughly practical soil preparation that makes it possible. The goal is to create soil that's easy to work, moisture-retentive, and full of organic matter—in short, the kind that makes gardeners drool and plants thrive.

It's the single most important thing you can do to stack the deck in your garden's favor, to get your plants off to an excellent start and keep them healthy. If instead you plant your roses in soil that's mostly clay, mostly sand, compacted, or all worn out, you won't get the results you want—no matter how healthy and disease-resistant the plants, no matter how assiduously you water and fertilize and wring your hands over them afterward.

But don't let this scare you. Soil preparation isn't at all complicated—it just requires a little sweat. Unless you're one of the lucky few blessed with naturally fabulous soil, you'll probably have to improve its texture and add organic matter. This part of the book will tell you how to do that and then how to plant the lovely roses you can't wait to grow.

The Lowdown on Dirt

What is soil, anyway? The short answer, as far as the average gardener is concerned, is that it's the medium through which roses receive the water and nutrients (chemicals such as nitrogen, phosphorus, and potassium) they need to survive. A few garden plants seem utterly unconcerned about soil quality, blooming away wherever they're planted; others, including roses, are generally choosier about growing conditions, although species, or "wild," roses and their close relatives are less particular.

The Right Stuff

All soils are made up of particles of clay, sand, and silt, in varying proportions, depending on where you live. Soil also contains water and organic matter—the decaying remains of plants and animals. And although we think of soil as solid, air is an essential component too, since plants' roots need oxygen to survive. In a good soil, in fact, about half the volume comes from mineral and organic matter, the other half from air and water, which occupy the tiny gaps, or pore spaces, between solid particles.

Where soil is concerned, the happy medium, so to speak, is what's called loam: a well-draining yet moisture-retaining combination of sand, clay, and silt. The mix of these three kinds of mineral particles—coupled with the amount of organic matter present—establishes how your soil handles water and how much oxygen can get to plants' roots. It also helps determine what's called soil tilth: how easy or difficult a soil is to dig and how readily roots can grow in it.

Organic matter plays a major part in the equation even though it may make up only 5 percent of a good soil. That decaying plant and animal matter—provided by roots, leaves, earthworm castings, the bodies of insects, and so on—turns into humus, which gives soil a nice dark color and from your plants' point of view constitutes manna from heaven. Humus improves the tilth of hard-to-work soils, helps soil hold on to moisture, and makes it easier for water to enter the soil in the first place. It also enhances the soil's capacity to attract, hold, and release nutrients as roots need them.

Roses, like many garden perennials, need a rich, well-draining soil if they're to reach their peak. Roses love water but can't stand "wet feet"—that is, having their roots sit around in soggy soil. If the soil is heavy clay, it'll tend to stay wet and soggy during rainy weather yet will bake hard and dry as brick in summer heat. If the soil is too sandy, rapid drainage is no problem but water passes through so quickly that the roots can't get as much moisture as they need. That's why the texture of the soil can mean the difference between your roses getting too much water or too little.

It's not difficult to figure out your soil's predominant texture. On a day when the soil is moist but not overly wet (one to several days after a significant rain), take a shovel or hand trowel and go to the spot where you've decided to plant your roses. Dig out about a handful of soil.

Look at the clump of dirt. What color is it? Generally speaking, deep brown and black soils are high in humus and usually need less amending. Clay soils—the most common kind—are often yellowish or reddish. Sandy soils tend to be pale in color. If the soil has a dull, grayish look, drainage in that area may be poor, creating a soil that's chronically waterlogged. Mottled soil often means that waterlogging is a problem at certain times of year.

Rub the soil between your fingers, then squeeze and roll it into a ball. How does it feel? Sandy soil has a loose, grainy texture and doesn't cling together. Its particles are the biggest of soil's mineral components, and because they don't pack together well, pore spaces are large, allowing water to move quickly through it. Silty soil is fine and smooth to the touch but not sticky and will form a loose, crumbly ball. Moist clay will roll into a ball or rope and keep its shape; wet clay feels very slick. Clay soils are made of tiny particles that readily jam together, especially when lubricated with water. That's why compaction—and the consequent loss of pore space—can be such a big problem in clay.

If your soil is quite sandy, you'll want to add lots of organic matter such as compost, aged manure, or peat moss in order to improve the soil's retention of water and nutrients. If your soil is mostly clay, you should add organic matter and sand, which will aerate it, help it drain more quickly, and correct its heavy texture. You may wish to add topsoil to both sandy and clay soils—a fast way to improve large quantities of poor soil. If the soil is dark, readily breaks apart, and is easy to dig, you may need only to fluff it up a bit.

How much amendment should you add? There's no one right answer or magic formula. Use your common sense, and add as much as it takes to make the soil crumbly and easy to dig. If your soil is already good, that might be as little as 5 percent of the given soil volume; if your soil is poor, consider replacing 25 to 30 percent of it with amendments. Don't be stingy. After all, you dig a given rose bed only once, and the results you get are proportionate to what you put into your soil. You won't regret the time invested in completing this task well, and both you and your roses will reap the rewards for many seasons.

The Soil Test

Before you start digging, there's one more thing you need to do: get a soil test.

The basic test will tell you the soil's pH (how acidic or alkaline it is), its levels of essential plant nutrients potassium and phosphorus, and how much fertilizer you'll need to correct any deficiencies and feed your roses. You can also request that your soil be tested for the percentage of organic matter, and—if for any reason you suspect other deficiencies—its levels of calcium, magnesium, and micronutrients such as iron, manganese, boron, zinc, copper, and molybdenum. These additional tests will cost a few dollars more, and for most people the basic test is sufficient. Be sure to specify the "crop" you intend to grow—roses in this case—so that the recommendations you receive are appropriate to your garden.

Just as all plants have preferences for sun or shade, moist soil or dry, and cool climates or warm, they also require soil in a specific range along the acid-to-alkaline continuum—that is, with a specific pH value. Roses are happiest at a pH around 6.0 to 6.5, or slightly acidic. A pH of 7 indicates a neutral soil; lower numbers are acidic, and higher numbers are alkaline. High-rainfall areas of the country (much of the eastern and coastal United States) tend to be acidic, whereas western soils are often alkaline.

The pH value is important to plants because a soil that's too acidic ("sour") or too alkaline ("sweet") can reduce the availability of nutrients, even if they are plentiful in the soil. An overly acidic soil ties up nitrogen, potassium, calcium, phosphorus, and magnesium. In alkaline soils phosphorus, iron, copper, zinc, boron, and manganese become less available.

If your soil is too acidic, the test results will recommend that you add one form or another of lime to sweeten things up. If the soil's too sweet already, you should add sulfur. The results will specify how much and what formulation to use per one hundred square feet of garden and how often to apply it. By getting the test before you plant, you'll be able to begin improving the soil's pH while you're digging in other soil amendments. Since it may take time—as much as three to four months—for the pH change to occur, it's best to do this the fall before spring planting or the spring before fall planting. But if you're in a rush, make the recommended pH corrections and plant. The lime or sulfur you've added won't harm newly planted roses.

Note that almost everything that happens in your garden—your use of fertilizers, fungicides, and amendments, even the amount of rainfall—will affect the pH. For that reason, it's wise to have the pH checked every year or two. You may want to consider buying pH-testing strips so you can assess the situation yourself each fall, with enough time to make corrections by spring.

Best of all, the benefits of a basic soil test far outweigh its cost—often less than ten dollars if it's performed by your county Agricultural Extension Service (usually listed under Agricultural Extension Service or Cooperative Extension Service in the county government section or the white pages of the phone book) or the state USDA soil-testing lab. If your state is one of the few that do not offer soil testing to consumers (call your county agent to find out), check the laboratories listing in the Yellow Pages for commercial labs that perform the same service. Your soil test may cost more but will be every bit as helpful.

Ready to test? Call your county agricultural extension agent or a commercial lab, and request a soil-test kit. You will get instructions on how to obtain, mix, and mail the sampled soil and often a small cardboard box to pack it in. On the instruction sheet you should indicate what tests you want performed.

To get good results, you'll need to take small quantities of soil from ten to fifteen random spots within the area that will become your rose bed. Dig your samples on a day when the soil is dry; if the soil isn't perfectly dry when you collect samples, let it dry before you mail it.

Using a clean hand trowel or garden spade, dig to a depth of about 6 inches in the sampling areas, and from the side of the hole collect a 1-inch-thick "slice" that represents the soil from top to bottom. Place your samples in a clean bucket or other container. Remove all trash, rocks, and plant matter from the soil. When you've collected all the samples, mix them thoroughly, and—presuming the soil is dry—pack and mail your soil and he testing fee according to the instructions provided. While you wait for the results, why not start looking through part 3 and choosing your favorite roses?

The hardest part about selecting soil amendments is that you've got so many choices, and each has something to recommend it. The goal is loose, rich, workable loam, and in order to get it you may need to correct the texture (making it lighter or heavier) and add organic matter. Bottom line: choose amendments that are within your budget and readily available. To buy in bulk and save money, shop at a feed store or agricultural co-op. Lime, sulfur, fertilizer, and other essentials are almost always cheaper there than at a nursery or home-improvement center.

Peat moss. Adding peat is an effective traditional method of increasing a soil's organic content and water-holding capacity. It's especially helpful if your soil is quite sandy. Dug from vast peat bogs in Canada, Michigan, and elsewhere, peat is somewhat expensive. It makes soil more acidic, so don't use peat if yours already tends to be sour.

Manure. Farmers have manured their gardens for hundreds of years—since long before the advent of soil tests and commercial fertilizers. An excellent amendment for any soil, manure contains small amounts of nitrogen (usually $1/2$ to 1 percent) along with loads of organic matter. Make sure the manure is composted (aged); fresh manure can "burn" plant roots. You can buy aged manure in bags from agricultural-supply stores and garden centers, but it's usually cheaper if you can buy it by the truckload from a nearby horse, pig, chicken, sheep, or dairy farm. What you don't dig into the garden now can be added to your compost pile. By the way—well-aged manure has no unpleasant odor.

Sharp sand. Sand adds no nutrients or organic matter, but it does wonders for a heavy clay soil's texture and drainage. You can buy horticultural-grade or builders' sand at home-improvement centers or in quantity from suppliers of gravel and stone.

Compost. This catch-all term simply means decayed plant matter, and the quality of the compost is determined by its ingredients—typically a combination of brown, or carbon-rich, plant material (for example, shredded dead leaves, shredded newspaper, straw, fallen pine needles) and green, or nitrogen-rich, material (for example, grass clippings, coffee grounds, vegetable peelings). Some people also add lime (especially if they're using pine needles or oak leaves) and nitrogen fertilizer to their compost to reduce acidity and hasten decomposition.

It's easy to create a compost pile in your backyard, and doing so is a good, cheap way to generate a steady supply of organic matter for your soil, whether it's heavy clay that needs lightening or sand that needs greater moisture-holding ability. To begin, buy or build composting bins or create a pile in an out-of-the-way part of the yard. To prevent odors, build the pile atop a 6- to 10-inch layer of brush so air can reach the bottom, and turn the ingredients (layers of green and brown materials) at least once a month. Keep it moist to speed decomposition. With a well-tended pile, you can have dark, crumbly, pleasant-smelling compost in a matter of months. If you'd like to learn more, read *Easy Compost: The Secret to Great Soil and Spectacular Plants* (New York: Brooklyn Botanic Garden, 1997), edited by Beth Hanson.

Mushroom compost: If you're lucky enough to have a mushroom farm in your area, you can buy this rich organic amendment directly from the grower. Although mushroom farmers use this medium (composed of various mixtures of straw, manure, cottonseed meal, brewer's grain, peat moss, and gypsum) to raise a single crop of mushrooms and then discard it, it's still plenty good for your soil. When you buy mushroom compost, ask the seller what the material's pH is and whether it is high in salts. If the pH is out of whack, you can correct it with lime or sulfur. If the compost is high in salts, however, it's best to let it sit outside for a year, turning the pile at least once, so the salts can leach out as rain percolates through. If you live in a low-rainfall area, water the pile thoroughly every couple of weeks.

Topsoil: If your soil is sandy or clayey, you may want to buy supplemental topsoil by the bag or the truckload (see topsoil or soil in the Yellow Pages). Ideally it should be a dark and crumbly loam. Before you buy, be aware that any kind of dirt can be labeled topsoil—there are no government standards to protect the consumer. Ask to see and feel what you're buying beforehand.

Lime: If your soil is acidic, use lime to correct its pH so your plants can get the nutrients they need. Your soil-test results will tell you what kind and how much to buy as well as how often to apply it. You can dig it into the rose bed now and apply it to the surface of the bed later, as needed.

Sulfur: Elemental sulfur makes soil more acidic. Again, the soil-test results will tell you whether you need it and how much to use. Follow the recommendations precisely: a little sulfur goes a long way.

Gypsum: You will need calcium sulfate, or gypsum, if your soil is quite high in sodium, as some western soils are. Such soils often have a salty crust on top, and if you suspect that describes your dirt, ask the soil-testing lab to check the sodium level. Gypsum helps the soil release sodium, which can then be flushed from the soil with water. Gypsum also helps clay soils become more crumbly and easier to work.

Dig It

Now we come to the spadework, literally—preparing the soil and a garden bed or individual planting holes for your roses. You can start by figuring out whether you need to prepare an entire bed or just dig good-size holes.

Two factors come into play: the number of bushes you intend to plant and how good the soil is to begin with. You will probably be better off digging a bed if you want to plant quite a few roses in a single section of your garden or if your soil is especially heavy.

If the soil in the planting area is compacted or heavy in clay and you plug your roses into planting holes full of excellent dirt, few of the roses' roots will ever leave those holes and work their way into the surrounding soil. And when it rains, water won't drain well from the loose soil in the holes into the nearby clay. You may as well plant the bushes in pots without drainage holes.

But if you're starting with only a few bushes and plan to add them to an existing bed with decent soil, it's easier to dig individual holes and improve the soil in those spots.

There are two other options to consider as well: building a raised bed and planting in pots. Raised beds are especially good for those who can't perform the hard labor of digging or who have extremely heavy soil or severe drainage problems. Growing roses in containers is a wise move for those who live in apartments, want to grow just a few roses, or have poorly draining soil. For more information, see page 31.

- A hand trowel and bucket for collecting soil samples.
- Lime, flour, a garden hose, or spray paint to mark the borders of the bed.
- A sharp spade to cut the perimeter of the bed, remove the sod, and loosen the soil (and if possible, a partner to help with sod removal). If there's a great deal of sod to remove, consider renting a gas-powered sod cutter.
- Roundup™ or another glyphosphate-based herbicide if you'd prefer killing the grass to removing it.
- A spading fork (a spade-size fork with long flat tines) for loosening soil and mixing in amendments.
- Amendments (organic matter, sand, lime, etc.) to improve the soil.
- A wheelbarrow or heavy tarpaulin to haul away and store excess soil.
- A garden rake for removing rocks and finishing the bed.
- For those digging individual planting holes, a large bucket or a wheelbarrow in which to mix and amend the soil.
- Five-gallon buckets or large tubs in which to soak bare-root roses before planting.
- Sturdy work gloves to protect your hands. Leather ones will do double duty as pruning gloves (see part 4 for more details).
- Bypass pruning shears for trimming damaged roots and canes (see part 4 for information on choosing a good pair of shears).
- Mulch to spread over the bed after planting.
- One or more soaker hoses (if you're planting more than a few roses and don't already have an irrigation system).

How to Dig a Garden Bed

The first step is to kill or remove any grass or weeds in the chosen area. Quick ways to do that are applying Roundup™, a fast-acting and environmentally friendly herbicide, and removing the turf with a sharp spade or sod lifter. If you go the Roundup™ route, you'll need to wait at least seven days before planting. After that, the active ingredient, glyphosphate, will have broken down into phosphate and the amino acid glycine in the soil and will pose no danger to the roses or other plants.

If you have the time and want to eliminate the work involved in turf removal, you can build a large compost heap atop the spot, wait six months or so for the pile to smother the grass, and then dig or till the compost into the soil. Be aware that some grasses—notably Bermuda grass, which grows from very long rhizomes—are hard to kill with passive methods.

When should you dig? If you plan to plant in spring, fall is a great time because the soil isn't frozen or waterlogged, as it may be in early spring, and the bed will have a chance to "ripen" for several months, giving soil microbes from the organic matter you've added a chance to multiply and spread throughout the soil. There they perform the important job of breaking down organic matter and making its nutrients available.

Of course, you can dig in the spring, once the weather warms and the soil is malleable. If the ground is wet, wait until it's had a chance to dry for several days. You don't want to remove heavy wet sod, and you should never dig or till when the soil is wet. If you do, you'll damage the soil's texture and encourage the formation of clods, large chunks of soil that are very difficult to break up. Slightly moist soil is best.

Start the process of creating your rose bed by marking its borders with a garden hose, rope or twine, a line of agricultural lime or flour slowly released from your hand, or even white spray paint. If you're planning to remove the turf rather than kill it, use a sharp spade, and cut neatly along the border edge.

Now, kneeling with a spade in hand, slice the turf away from the soil beneath it a section at a time, leaving behind as much topsoil as possible but making sure to get all the grass and weed roots. If you're careful, you'll be able to roll up strips of turf as you go. The process is a lot easier if you can recruit a partner: one of you can slice while the other rolls the turf.

If you're planning an especially large rose bed, you might consider renting a sod cutter, a self-propelled gas-powered tool that cuts the turf into foot-wide strips. Or, if you're planning lots of turf stripping in the future, you can buy a hand-powered sod cutter from a horticultural-supply company or garden center.

If the sod you've removed is healthy and thick, you can use it to patch bare or weedy areas of your lawn. If you don't need it, turn it grass side down and stack it on the compost pile. Cover with soil or compost and let it rot.

1. Before you start, bring the shape of your flower bed to mind, and mentally mark it off into a series of trenches, each about a foot wide and as long as the bed. You will prepare the soil in each trench in two stages (hence the term "double-digging"), one trench at a time, until the entire bed is finished. here's how it works: With your spade, dig the first trench about as deep as the tool's blade, piling the soil into a wheelbarrow or onto a tarpaulin.

2. Continue working in this first trench, loosening the soil another spade's depth with that tool or—better still—a spading fork. Mix in amendments, and leave this second layer of loosened soil in place.

3. Loosen and dig a second trench to one spade's depth. Move the loosened soil into the first trench, and work in amendments. Now loosen the deeper soil in trench number two, but leave it in place, after incorporating amendments. Keep going, always moving the top layer of soil into the previously made trench and leaving the deeper layer in place.

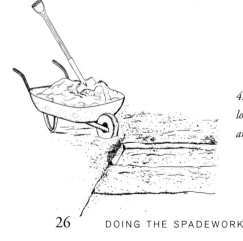

4. When you get to the final trench, fill it with the loosened soil you took from trench number one, and amend it as needed.

Now it's time to dig or till the soil and incorporate amendments. Gather all your tools and amendments by the flower-bed-to-be. You can use the tarpaulin or wheelbarrow as a repository for the dirt you're removing. After all, you will be adding amendments, because you're going to end up with more soil than you started with. A freshly dug bed will settle with time and rainfall, so you should try to create a bed that's slightly mounded. You can use the excess soil to fill any low spots in the yard or add it to your compost pile.

One excellent—though labor-intensive—traditional method of preparing a bed is called "double-digging" (see the illustration on page 26). If your soil is pretty decent already, you don't need to double-dig, but this technique does a world of good for heavy clay or compacted soils.

An easier way to prepare the bed, especially if your soil is fairly decent, is to loosen the soil to a depth of about 18 inches, remove excess soil, spread the amendments evenly over the bed, and mix them in with a spading fork or tiller. As you mix, avoid burying the topsoil and amendments.

You're almost done when the amendments are evenly mixed, the soil is loose and fine-textured, and there are no large clods. You can rake out and dispose of stubborn clods and rocks. Finish by raking the surface smooth but slightly mounded. Once the bed is prepared, keep off it: walking on that lovely loose soil will compact it, undoing some of your hard work and eliminating some of the pore spaces that hold air and water.

How to Dig a Planting Hole

If you decide not to prepare an entire garden bed, you'll prepare a "minibed" for each rose. An old saw says you should dig a hole twice as big as a lazy person would dig. That's a quaint way of saying you shouldn't skimp. The hole should be wider than it is deep—about 24 inches wide and 18 inches deep—because that's the way a rose's roots grow. Space the holes far enough apart that your roses won't become overcrowded.

As you dig each hole, set the soil aside in a large bucket or wheelbarrow or anyplace else you can mix in the amendments. Once you've done so and the soil is loose and fine, dump or shovel it back into the hole if you're not ready to plant, and avoid walking on the planting areas afterward. The soil should be somewhat mounded to accommodate settling.

Get 'Em in the Ground

Finally, it's time to plant. The hard work's all done—this part is simplicity itself.

Bare-root Roses

Before planting, soak bare-root bushes in 5-gallon buckets or large tubs of water for 8 to 24 hours. Some rose growers prefer to use muddy water; some add hormone-and-vitamin products that are supposed to jump-start plant growth; others add 1 cup household bleach per 5 gallons water during the last minute of soaking in order to foil any lurking fungi and bacteria. Plain water works fine too. After the soaking, trim off any damaged or mildewed-looking roots with clean, sharp pruning shears. Trim any broken canes, remove any that look unhealthy or dried out, and prune to achieve a balance of canes to root mass. Canes should be no longer than 12 inches.

A WELL-PLANTED BARE-ROOT ROSE

1. Dig a hole about 24 inches wide and 18 inches deep in a prepared bed (or amend just the soil within the hole).

2. Determine how deep to plant the bed union, given your region's winters.

3. Form a mound of soil in the hole, and spread the roots around it.

4. When the bud union is at the ideal depth, fill the hole halfway, and firm the plant with your hands. Water well. When the water drains, add the rest of the soil, firm the plant, and water again.

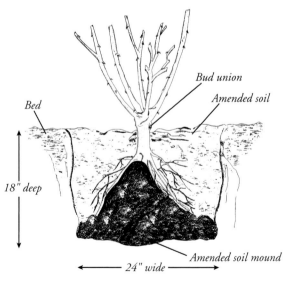

Bud union

Bed

Amended soil

18" deep

Amended soil mound

24" wide

Now dig holes (18 inches deep, 24 inches wide) in your newly prepared flower bed or excavate the individual holes you've dug.

How deep should you plant your roses? The crucial question is where to situate what's called the bud union—below ground, at ground level, or above ground. In grafted roses, the bud union is the knobby area where the rose variety you wanted was grafted to the plant's understock, a root system from any of several vigorous varieties. Roses grown on their own roots should be planted at the same depth they were grown in the field. (You'll be able to tell from the color change on the main stem.)

There are lots of opinions about planting depth, but the determining factor is your climate. The colder your winters, the deeper you should plant. The surrounding soil will help insulate the bud union, providing some protection against winter-kill. Gardeners in Zones 4 and 5 (see the USDA Plant Hardiness Zone Map on page 160) typically site the bud union 2, 3, or even 4 inches below ground; those in Zone 6 may plant at ground level or an inch or two below (especially if the rose in question isn't particularly hardy); those in warmer climates usually keep the graft at ground level or an inch or two above

because it is believed that sunlight helps stimulate the growth of basal breaks (new canes) from the bud union.

If you're in doubt, check with your local rose society or an American Rose Society consulting rosarian (see the appendix for information on finding a consulting rosarian).

Once you've made the depth decision, pull your bare-root bush from the tub where it's been soaking. Locate the bud union so you can determine how deep to plant. Put some amended soil back into the

The soil mounded around these newly planted roses helps protect them from cold and keeps canes moist.

planting hole, forming a cone or mound in the center. Now spread the roots around the cone. Check the depth by laying a spade or piece of lumber flat across the planting hole: it will give you a visual indicator of the soil's ultimate level so you can judge whether the bud union is where you want it. If the rose is in too deep, remove it, add more soil, and build a new cone. If the hole is too shallow, take out the rose, and dig more deeply.

When the rose is at the perfect depth, fill in the hole about halfway, using your gloved hands to firm the soil around the rose's roots. Don't be timid—your rose is tougher than you may think, and it's important to get rid of air pockets (despite the importance of tiny air-filled pore spaces, large air pockets can kill roots). Now muddy it in by watering quite thoroughly, till the water nearly reaches the top. Let the water drain away, add more soil, and firm the plant again with your hands, thrusting them into the soil to eliminate air pockets. You want the rose to be well-seated in its new home.

Now use your hands to build a soil ring (about an inch high) around the perimeter of the planting hole. That will encourage water to soak into the hole and not drain away. Water again thoroughly.

Finally, presuming you're planting in late winter or early spring, take some loose soil or mulch and gently mound it around the newly planted rose to a height of 8 to 12 inches. The mound will protect the rose's growth points from cold, drying winds. Over the next few weeks, as the weather warms, use a hose to gradually and gently wash away the mound. Avoid brushing the soil or mulch away; it's easy to break off tender new growth.

Container-grown and Boxed Roses

Planting containerized roses is even easier. Locate the bud union and determine how deeply to plant (see the discussion of this point in the previous section). Then scoop some soil from the intended site, unpot the rose, tease apart the roots if the plant is root-bound, and plant the rose at the appropriate depth, firming the soil with your hands. Incidentally, container-grown roses can be planted any time the ground isn't frozen, although you'll need to water often—probably daily in well-drained soils—for several weeks if you plant during the summer. Early fall is a great time to plant containerized roses, though it may be hard to find them in garden centers.

If you've purchased "plant-them-box-and-all" roses, you can do just that, following the package instructions. Bury the entire container—edges that protrude from the soil can wick moisture away from the rose. Or, as some gardeners prefer, you can cut the plants from their packaging with a razor blade and treat them as though they were bare-root plants. (Don't attempt this unless the roses are still leafless and dormant.)

Planting in Raised Beds . . .

The beauty of gardening aboveground or in pots is that creating good soil is a snap. Instead of starting with heavy clay or sand and expending all the effort necessary to transform it, you just bring in good soil and fill the container, whether it's a 2-foot-high 4- by 25-foot raised bed or a 15-gallon plastic pot. Raised beds are a good option for those whose soil is rocky or extremely poor or who don't have the time or strength to dig. They're also ideal for gardeners confined to a wheelchair or those who want to eliminate the back strain involved in bending and stooping to weed and tend a garden. Build the bed narrow enough to permit reaching the middle from either side.

Other advantages include excellent drainage, fewer weeds (if you bring in clean soil), and no compaction. After all, you're not going to walk around on the soil surface. Because raised beds drain rapidly, plants require more frequent watering and fertilization.

Raised-bed kits, consisting of plastic borders and metal hardware to connect the plastic and anchor it to the soil, are available from garden centers and mail-order catalogs, but most don't allow building a bed that's deep enough for roses—ideally 18 inches to 2 feet or more. The deeper the bed, the more room there is for roses' roots but the more you'll pay for soil and construction materials. The shallower the bed, the more you'll have to dig into the soil below to give roses ample room to put down roots. If the soil below is compacted, break it up before building the bed atop it.

Good border materials include pressure-treated wood, landscape timbers, railroad ties, concrete blocks (which you can camouflage with acrylic paint or stain), and planks of redwood, cypress, or cedar. Concrete and pressure-treated wood rated for ground contact won't rot even in hot, wet climates.

. . . and Containers

But maybe you don't have a yard of your own—or perhaps you've already filled the available garden space to the bursting point. By planting in con-

Miniatures such as 'Millie Walters' make fine container plants—but so do full-size roses, as long as the pots are large enough.

tainers, you can grow roses on a terrace, deck, or driveway or place the pots in any sunny spot you like.

Good drainage is critical to successfully growing roses in containers. Use a good commercial potting mix rather than garden soil, and make sure your containers have drainage holes. It's not necessary to use saucers, which can trap moisture in the pot and cause root rot. Some rosarians add perlite or sand to the mix to ensure that the medium has adequate pore space.

Plastic pots work well because they're durable, economical, and lightweight. They also need watering less frequently than clay pots. In hot weather you may need to water daily—perhaps twice a day—depending on the heat and the volume of soil in the pot. Check containers each day, and adjust your watering as needed. The soil should be consistently moist but never soggy. To help the potting mix retain moisture without becoming waterlogged, mix in a small quantity of water-holding polymer crystals, available at garden centers. The crystals swell as they're hydrated and keep water available to roots for a longer time.

Select generously sized wide pots to give roots adequate room, provide greater insulation from heat and cold, and reduce the frequency of watering. Ten- to 15-gallon containers work well for hybrid teas, grandifloras, floribundas, shrubs, and other good-size roses; 7- to 10-gallon pots for most polyanthas and small shrubs. Miniatures will ultimately need 5- to 7-gallon pots, although you needn't start them in such large containers.

You will need to fertilize more often to compensate for the rapidly draining medium, the small soil volume, and the fact that roots can't stretch out in search of nutrients. Many experts recommend feeding containerized roses with a dilute solution of water-soluble fertilizer or an organic tea of manure or fish emulsion every two to four weeks, although you can use regular granular fertilizer, watered in well, if you prefer.

Disadvantages of growing roses in containers include the sheer weight of the pots—if you ever need to move them—and, for those in colder climates, the difficulty of providing winter protection. When winter comes, you'll need to store your potted roses in an unheated cellar, shed, or garage where the temperature is low enough to ensure dormancy but won't dip below freezing; sink the pots into the ground; bury the plants in the compost pile; or surround the pots with a generous supply of leaves or mulch, perhaps adding a burlap covering. If the roses are tender and you live in a cold climate, complete coverage with soil may be necessary to keep them alive.

WHAT TO EXPECT IN A ROSE'S FIRST SEVERAL SEASONS

Given ordinary care, plenty of sunshine, and good soil, any good-quality rose will ultimately reach its potential and begin repaying your investment. It doesn't happen overnight, though.

Grafted grade 1 roses usually attain full size by the second growing season after planting—perhaps by the end of their first season if they're rapid growers, your area is blessed with a long season, or they were planted the previous fall. The newly planted rose's first task is to produce roots so that nutrients and water can be readily taken up, and planting in fall gives them extra time to settle in and grow roots before the demands of flowering begin.

Depending on the plant, roses growing on their own roots may take three to five seasons to gain full size or put on much of a show. The difference is due to the slower root development of many cultivated varieties—and to the fact that own-root plants you buy are usually much smaller than grade 1 grafted bushes. The vigorous rose strains used as rootstocks, in contrast, take off like a rocket, driving rapid top growth.

Own-root roses may bloom sparsely or not at all for the first several years. The same is true of climbers, which often do not flower until their second or third summer. Don't let your eagerness for armloads of blooms dissuade you from choosing these delayed-gratification roses. Go ahead and plant them, knowing that your patience will be rewarded.

Taking Care of Your New Plants: Watering and Mulching

Now you've planted a rosebush or a whole rose garden. Before you put away the tools and go inside with a well-exercised back and an inner glow, take the time to lay down a soaker hose—the cheapest irrigation system you can buy—and spread a generous layer of mulch. You'll greatly reduce the weed population, keep the soil moist, and save yourself hours of labor in the growing season ahead. (For more information on watering, see part 4.)

As soon as your plants are in the ground, grab your soaker hose (or hoses, depending on the size of the bed), and start unrolling it onto the lawn. Once you've uncurled the entire length of the hose, go along the rose bed and encircle each rose two or three times, keeping the open end of the hose closer to the water supply. Or you can run the hose in zigzagged rows between the plants. The point is to position the hose where it can deliver the most water to your roses with the least waste.

Once that's done, you're ready to mulch your roses, covering the soaker hose at the same time. Doing so will make the soaker last longer and improve the appearance of your rose bed. Leave the open end of the hose above the mulch so it's easy to locate and doesn't fill up with mulch and soil. If you live in a mild climate, you can leave soakers in place year-round. If not, they'll last longer if you take them up in late fall and reinstall them in spring.

Many kinds of material make good mulch, so the decision depends largely on what's available and economical and looks good to you. The cheapest option is homemade compost, presuming you have a large enough supply and your compost pile is hot enough to destroy weed seeds. Dark, fine compost, screened to remove large particles, makes a good-looking mulch and continuously adds organic matter to your soil as it breaks down, but because it degrades rapidly, you have to replenish it frequently.

Pine needles make a good, though acidic, mulch and are an excellent option if you can get large quantities cheaply or free and your soil's not overly acidic to start with.

A reasonably priced option is composted bark or wood chips. In order to reduce landfill use, many communities have begun grinding and composting yard waste such as brush and leaves. Call your city's solid-waste department to find out whether your area has such a program. Composted yard waste makes nice dark mulch, and the price is much lower than what you'd pay a landscaping service for wood chips or bark mulch. This composted mulch is typically sold by the truckload and will cost more if you must have it delivered.

If composted yard waste isn't available, call local landscaping services and compare their prices for bark mulch. Bark can be bought by the bag at garden centers, but pound for pound it costs a great deal more than when purchased in bulk. Landscapers also sell cocoa hulls as mulch, and they make an attractive and fragrant topping for your flower beds, although the price is usually higher than for bark.

Keep in mind that if you use wood mulch of any kind, it should be aged, not freshly ground, and you'll need to use slightly more nitrogen when you fertilize. The natural process that breaks down wood (or any form of organic matter) takes a certain amount of nitrogen from the soil, so you will have to compensate.

Some people use fine gravel or crushed stone as mulch. Although it lasts virtually forever, it's less effective at holding weeds at bay. It's also a very expensive mulch, and it obviously won't add organic matter to the soil.

Mulch your rose bed 1 to 2 inches deep. If your climate is hot or quite dry, use the higher amount so you can conserve as much soil moisture as possible.

All you have to do now is keep your newly planted roses moist. For the first couple of weeks, water deeply every three or four days (if you plant in summer, daily watering may be necessary). After that, water deeply at least once a week—more often if the weather is dry or the plants look stressed or dried out. Once roses are established, they can usually get by on an inch or two of water a week, supplied by rainfall or gardener. Bear in mind that although roses despise soggy soil, they love moisture and perform best if you don't allow them to dry out.

Now you've done all the hard work—it's time to sit back and wait for the flower show to begin.

the rose gallery

The Essentials

In this part you'll learn more about the various categories of roses, both old and new, and find descriptions of one hundred excellent roses, most of which have good disease-resistance, making them fine choices for beginning rose gardeners or those who would prefer to spend less time battling fungal diseases.

Disease-resistance depends on many factors, not just a plant's inherited ability to fight fungi: the health of the specimen, your climate (temperature, level of rainfall, relative humidity), your cultural practices, and the planting site, to name a few. Bear in mind that some climates are more challenging than others. For example, the disease commonly known as blackspot can germinate only on wet leaflets. That means gardeners in high-rainfall regions will have more trouble from blackspot than those in dry climates, no matter how healthy their roses. Nobody gets off the hook entirely, though; gardeners in drier areas may not need to worry about blackspot, but they can't ignore powdery mildew, a fungus that's actually discouraged by water on the leaflet surface.

And fungal diseases can come in various forms, each of which affects a plant differently. For example, when researchers in warm, wet Mississippi inoculated thirty-nine old-rose cultivars with seven different isolates, or variants, of blackspot, some cultivars shucked off all infection (the alba 'Félicité Parmentier', the damask 'Mme. Hardy', the centifolia 'The Bishop', and the gallica 'Rosa Mundi'), some were infected by one or more variants but not others, and several were infected by all seven. Even those that proved invulnerable in that test might well be susceptible to other variants in different locales. Furthermore, diseases can develop a resistance to overused fungicides.

Despite these caveats, most of the varieties described in these pages have a reputation for good to better-than-average disease-resistance. Most have also received high scores—8.0 and above—from members of the American Rose Society (ARS) throughout the United States. A score of 6.0 to 6.9 indicates the rose's performance is "fair"; 7.0 to 7.9 means "good"; 8.0 to 8.9 is "excellent"; and 9.0 to 9.9 means "outstanding." (All ratings cited are from the ARS's *1998 Handbook for Selecting Roses*. Ratings can and often do change over time.)

Think of this limited selection of one hundred cultivars as a starting point in your introduction to roses. Hundreds of other good roses are also listed by name (along with the numerical rating and color category the ARS has assigned them) and are definitely worth reading about and considering for your garden. But don't stop there: the universe of available varieties numbers in the thousands, and if you like a rose and it performs to your satisfaction, it's the right choice for you.

The Wide World of Roses

If you're new to roses, the plants you're most likely to have seen and heard about are hybrid teas, floribundas, grandifloras, and miniatures: colorful repeat-blooming plants available at every garden center and in dozens of catalogs. But these are only four of the most modern classes of roses, none of which existed before 1867, the year usually accepted as marking the introduction of the first hybrid tea. Beautiful as these roses are, you'll shortchange yourself if you don't also consider roses from earlier days.

Roses fall into many classes, and a basic grasp of this classification system will help you understand the differences among various kinds of roses. For example, hybrid teas and floribundas are classes of modern repeat-blooming roses. Albas, damasks, and gallicas are once-blooming old European roses. The shrub group covers a wide range of roses with an incredible variety of sizes, flower shapes, and growth habits. Most are repeat-blooming. Classes differ a great deal in winter hardiness, disease-resistance, growth habit, flower form, and so on.

Interestingly, it's the date of the class's creation, not the year the specific variety was introduced, that determines whether a rose is old or modern. Gallicas, for example, the most ancient Western roses in cultivation, are believed to have been grown since before the time of Christ. The rose 'James Mason', although it was introduced in 1982, is a gallica too—and hence an old garden rose (OGR)—because its parents are gallicas.

In most cases old garden roses, also called heritage, antique, or heirloom roses, look quite different from modern roses: their blooms are often fuller, flatter, and softer in color. They're usually prized for the look of their full-blown mature flowers, whereas hybrid teas and grandifloras are considered most beautiful as their high-centered (see the sidebar on page 41 for a definition) buds are opening. Some OGRs bloom more than once a season, as nearly all modern roses do; others spend all their energy on one fabulous flowering in late spring or early summer. Don't ban the old European roses from your garden just because they flower only once a year. After all, if your garden makes room for irises, azaleas, forsythia, peonies, and other once-bloomers, why exclude roses?

And, as the noted British rosarian Graham Stuart Thomas points out, "the rose was originally a shrub"—not an everblooming flower machine but a bush to be planted in the garden alongside other shrubs, perennials, bulbs, annuals, and trees. Generally speaking, once-blooming roses become hard-working garden shrubs with good foliage and graceful lines after their flowers fade. So keep an open mind about roses of all kinds and the different kinds of beauty they can bestow on your garden.

You may find that as you learn more about roses you gravitate almost exclusively to old roses or to modern ones. Each kind has its diehard fans; and of course, some gardeners appreciate roses of all sorts. It really doesn't matter as long as you grow what appeals to you.

Understanding the Entries

Each plant portrait in the rose gallery includes the following information: the name of the cultivar, in single quotes; its class, according to the ARS; its ARS rating, if any (new roses, obscure varieties, and a number of old roses have not been rated); its ARS color classification; the name of the breeder or, in the case of sports (spontaneous genetic mutations), the introducer; and the year of introduction or registration, whichever came first. Code names and other names under which the rose may be sold are indicated. (The code identifies a plant's hybridizer or introducer, and it can be useful when a rose is sold under more than one cultivar name.) Following that, you'll find information about bloom form and color, scent, if any, foliage, winter-hardiness, growth habit, and in some cases other details about the rose's origins, awards, noteworthy characteristics, and so on.

If two hardiness zones are indicated, you can be sure a healthy specimen will be hardy in the higher-numbered zone. With moderate winter protection it should survive in the lower zone as well, especially where there's a long-lasting

Cupped   Blooms whose petals form a rounded, open cup.

Double   Blooms with twenty-four to fifty petals; very double blooms have more than fifty petals.

Eye or pip   A round, buttonlike center in a very double rose.

Globular   Flower shape in which petals curve toward the center, creating a rounded bloom.

High-centered   Flower shape in which a bud's inner petals are arranged in a pointed cone that tends to stay upright as the bloom unfurls.

Hip   The fruitlike ripened receptacle containing rose seeds.

Moss   Pine- or resin-scented glandular growth appearing on buds and stems.

Once-blooming   Having one period of bloom each growing season, in late spring or summer.

Pegging   Pinning long, flexible canes to the soil with wire in order to stimulate flower production all along the stems.

Prickles   Rose thorns.

Quartered   Flower shape in which a fully double bloom's petals are folded or arranged into distinct sections, or quarters. Most common in old European varieties.

Reflexed   Flower shape in which petals curve back and downward as the bloom opens, sometimes forming a fluffy ball.

Remontant   Twice-blooming or capable of repeat bloom.

Reverse   The back of the flower petal.

Rugose   Wrinkled—a term applied to foliage with deeply cut leaf veins.

Semidouble   Flowers with twelve to twenty-four petals, arranged in two or three rows.

Single   The simplest blooms, with only five to twelve petals. The stamens in the open bloom's center often play a major part in the appeal of single flowers.

Sport   A spontaneous genetic mutation. A branch that sports may have different-colored blooms, the ability to climb, the capacity for repeat-bloom, or other characteristics that distinguish it from the mother plant.

Stamens   The filaments and anthers that constitute the flower's male (pollen-bearing) reproductive organs.

snow cover and it is sheltered from drying winds, although it may suffer some cane dieback. With thorough winter protection rose growers in cold climates can successfully grow less-hardy roses such as hybrid teas. See part 4 for complete details.

Most of the plant portraits in this book say nothing about a variety's preference for sun because all roses are by nature sun-loving, typically preferring six hours or more per day. Roses that can tolerate some shade, getting by on four to five hours of sun, are highlighted, but less sunshine usually means fewer flowers and more problems with fungal diseases. You can try any rose in a less-sunny spot, then judge whether its performance is acceptable.

ARS COLOR CLASSIFICATIONS

The ARS has assigned most roses a specific color code. Some are relatively unambiguous (for example, deep pink or medium yellow). Others, specifically those including the word *blend*, cover any number of mixed color possibilities.

White (includes white, near white, and white blend)
Light yellow
Medium yellow
Deep yellow
Yellow blend
Apricot blend (includes apricot and apricot blend)
Orange blend (includes orange and orange blend)
Orange-pink (includes orange-pink and orange-pink blend)
Orange-red (includes orange-red and orange-red blend)
Light pink
Medium pink
Deep pink
Pink blend
Medium red
Dark red
Red blend
Mauve (includes mauve and mauve blend)
Russet

Old Roses

Species

The oldest of the old are the original species roses—those that evolved in various parts of the world without human intervention. Opinions vary, but many experts believe the number of rose species is about two hundred. These roses are by nature well-adapted to growing conditions in their native regions—that is, they're resistant to the diseases and pests common to the area where they evolved, hardy enough to survive the native winters, and able to make do with the amount of rainfall nature provides. This toughness doesn't necessarily apply, however, when species roses are planted in conditions quite different from those where they developed.

Many make attractive, easy-care garden plants and landscape shrubs and are especially well-suited to naturalistic gardens. Species roses are single, meaning they have just one row of petals (although some variants of species have semi-double or double flowers), but their simple blooms and graceful proportions give them a quiet beauty. Although most bloom just once a year, there are a few exceptions, including *Rosa rugosa*, *R. laxa*, and *R. chinensis* 'Viridiflora' (also called 'Green Rose'). Another asset of species roses is their ability to form hips, which add color and beauty late in the growing season and provide food for birds and small mammals. Elsewhere in this section you'll find a list of good species roses to consider.

Probably the most familiar species in commerce today is *R. rugosa*, admired for its spice-scented blooms, superior winter hardiness, adamant disease-resistance, and absolute ease of care. Because of these sterling traits—and *R. rugosa*'s repeat bloom—the species has been widely hybridized, creating a large class of hybrid rugosas. Descriptions of several excellent hybrids can be found in the shrub section.

The species Rosa glauca *is prized more for its purplish foliage than its small flowers.*

Old European Roses

The most venerable of the cultivated roses—the gallicas, damasks, albas, centifolias, and mosses—are typically very fragrant and cold-hardy, thriving as far north as USDA Zone 4 and in some cases Zone 3. They bloom generously just once each year, with rare exceptions, and come in white and various shades of pink, crimson, and (in the case of gallicas) purple. Unfortunately, the vast majority of old roses once in commerce have vanished. Although those that remain are unquestionably beautiful and valuable plants, it's impossible to say whether they represent the best of their classes.

These shrubby roses usually perform better in cooler climates; most suffer in the summer heat of Zone 8 and warmer parts. Not all old European roses are extremely disease-resistant, as popular articles often claim. Albas deserve that reputation, although they may get rust in coastal areas. Mosses, gallicas, damasks, and centifolias are susceptible to powdery mildew, and they may also get blackspot and rust. Nonetheless, old roses are typically tough customers that if well cared for can tolerate disease without a great loss of vigor.

Gallicas

The oldest cultivated Western roses, these derive from an ancient species rose, *Rosa gallica*, found in Europe and western Asia. The other four classes of old European roses descend in one way or another from *R. gallica*, named by the eighteenth-century Swedish taxonomist Carolus Linnaeus after Gaul, the ancient region corresponding to present-day France and Belgium. It wasn't a bad choice, as the French adopted and began raising gallicas on a large scale in the early 1800s. They weren't the first, however; English and Dutch nurserymen had been raising gallica seedlings as early as the 1600s. What we think of as hybridizing—intentionally crossing two different roses in order to achieve a specific goal—didn't begin until the late 1800s, with English farmer and cattle breeder Henry Bennett. Before then, new varieties were created when established ones sported (that is, when spontaneous genetic mutations took place) or natural crosses occurred between roses growing close together and seeds were planted (or sprouted on their own).

The flowers of most gallicas are held high, on firm stalks, and come in deep, rich colors; a few are blush or light pink. These shrubs are typically rounded and compact, with slender canes and small prickles. They're tolerant of poorer soils but perform better in rich ground. If grown on their own roots, most sucker freely. To keep them within bounds in a small garden, choose grafted plants.

Damasks

Legend has it that the damasks were brought to Europe from Damascus by knights returning from the Crusades. However it reached Europe, this ancient class may have been the result of a cross between a gallica and the species *R. phoenicea*. Larger and thornier than the gallicas, damasks are often sprawling in growth habit, with downy, grayish-green foliage. They form medium-size upright shrubs and have very prickly canes. Their

'Autumn Damask', the first repeat-blooming rose discovered in the Western world.

semidouble or double cup-shaped blooms come in soft pinks and whites rather than the intense shades of the gallicas and are strongly perfumed.

One very important and ancient damask—'Autumn Damask', or 'Quatre Saisons'—blooms twice. Some believe 'Autumn Damask' is the remontant (twice-blooming) rose mentioned by Virgil in the first century B.C.

Albas

Cultivated since the days of the Greeks and Romans, albas are believed to be the result of a natural cross between *Rosa gallica* and *R. canina*, the dog rose. Vigorous, upright, and often growing taller than 6 feet, albas were formerly nicknamed "tree roses." Their grayish-green leaflets are exceptionally disease-resistant.

Although albas' blooms come only in white and pale pink, their form and perfume are exquisite. Graham Stuart Thomas praises the members of this class as "supreme over all the other old roses in vigour, longevity, foliage, delicacy of colour . . . and purity of scent."

Centifolias and Mosses

The newest of the old European roses, centifolias and mosses were very popular during the Victorian era. Centifolias were appreciated for their very full, cabbagy, and somewhat droopy blooms. Their gaunt, prickly canes form lax, open shrubs with sparse foliage.

Mosses—so called because of the mossy, pine-scented growth that covers buds and stems—are sports from either centifolias or damask perpetuals (roses descended from 'Autumn Damask'). Those that sprang from the latter class have a second, if unimpressive, flowering in fall.

Rosa rugosa Clones

Rosa rugosa 'Alba', species, 9.3, white
R. rugosa 'Rubra', species, 9.3, mauve

Medium-size, silky, crinkled, single flowers of pure white or deep pink with creamy yellow stamens; strong spicy fragrance; repeat-blooming. Shiny dark-green rugose foliage; many small prickles; good autumn color. Hardy to Zone 2. Vigorous upright habit of 5–6 feet in height and spread; *R. rugosa* 'Alba' grows more densely.

Rosa rugosa *'Rubra', species.*

These species clones are among the most carefree roses in cultivation. Although individual clove-scented blooms don't last long, the plants make up for it with continuous repeat throughout the growing season, producing large orange-red hips in fall. Rugosas make good dense hedges and tolerate dry, poorer soil and some shade, although flowering is reduced. Many rugosas suffer in hot climates, but some Southern rosarians believe this problem can be overcome by grafting them onto a heat-tolerant rootstock such as 'Fortuniana' rather than growing them on their own roots.

Gallicas

'**Alain Blanchard**', gallica, 8.5, mauve, Vibert, 1839.

Large, rich purplish-crimson semidouble cupped blooms become mottled with a lighter shade of crimson, giving flowers a unique spotted appearance; very showy golden stamens; sweet fragrance; once-blooming. Hips form if plant is not deadheaded. Dense foliage is olive-green and disease-resistant; reddish prickles. Hardy to Zone 4. Bush is vigorous, reaching 4–5 feet in height and width. Tolerates some shade. Probably of mixed gallica and centifolia parentage. 'Alain Blanchard' tolerates warm Southern climates better than some gallicas.

'Alain Blanchard', gallica.

'**Belle de Crécy**', gallica, 8.1, mauve, Hardy, introduced in or before 1829.

Medium-size full, flat, very double blooms of cerise-pink and purple mature to a grayish lavender; flowers have green button eye; deliciously fragrant; once-blooming. Foliage is a dull grayish green and disease-resistant, although powdery mildew may develop; few prickles. Hardy to Zone 4. Compact, rounded bush reaches about 4 feet in height, 3 feet in width. This belle—named after Madame de Pompadour, mistress of Louis XV— is one of the most free-flowering gallicas.

'**Charles de Mills**', gallica, 8.6, mauve, date of introduction unknown.

Large, very full, flat, quartered dark crimson-purple blooms that turn maroon and grayish mauve as they mature; flowers have pale green pip; fragrant; once-blooming. Lush medium-green foliage; disease-resistant and less mildew-prone than some gallicas; few prickles. Hardy to Zone 4. A large, vigorous shrub reaching

'Charles de Mills', gallica.

4–5 feet in height. Makes a good hedge. English hybridizer and rosarian David Austin calls 'Charles de Mills' "the largest flowered and most spectacular of the old roses."

'Rosa Mundi', gallica, 9.0, pink blend, cultivated before 1581.
(A sport of 'Apothecary's Rose' ['Officinalis', or *Rosa gallica* 'Officinalis']. Also called *Rosa gallica* 'Versicolor'.)

'Rosa Mundi', gallica.

Striking large, semidouble blooms striped and splashed in white, pink, and rose-red, with glowing yellow stamens; fragrant; once-blooming, over a long season. Good for cutting. Forms red hips. Medium-green disease-resistant foliage; few prickles. Hardy to Zone 4. Reaches 3–4 feet in height and width. Described in print by herbalists as early as 1583 (although it may be much older), the free-flowering 'Rosa Mundi' remains one of the most popular and recognizable old garden roses. The best of shrubs, it mixes well in both formal and cottage gardens and makes an excellent low hedge. Sometimes a few flowers will revert to the solid light-crimson color of 'Apothecary's Rose', which was the center of a thriving industry in thirteenth-century Provins, a town southeast of Paris.

'Superb Tuscan', gallica, 8.5, mauve, cultivated before 1837.
(Thought to be a seedling or sport of 'Tuscany'. Also called 'Superb Tuscany' and 'Tuscany Superb'.)

Large, flat, velvety, cupped, double blooms of intense maroon-violet; fragrant; once-blooming. Dark-green disease-resistant foliage; few prickles. Hardy to Zone 4. A bushy, upright shrub of 3–5 feet in height. Good for cutting and as a hedge rose. Although 'Superb Tuscan' resembles its parent, the offspring is larger, with fuller and more double flowers. Its rich blooms are darkest in full sun.

Damasks

'Celsiana', damask, 8.8, light pink, cultivated before 1750.

Large, semidouble crinkled, silky blooms of pale pink with golden stamens, fading to blush, in clusters of three or four; richly fragrant, with notes of citrus and spice; once-blooming. Foliage is small, smooth, glossy, and grayish green; disease-resistant. Moderately prickly. Hardy to Zone 4. An upright shrub reaching 4–6 feet in height.

'Mme. Hardy', damask, 9.0, white, Hardy, 1832.

Large, full, flat, cupped, and quartered blooms of pure white with a green eye in the center, borne in clusters; lemony fragrance; once-blooming. Lush gray-green foliage; many prickles; moderately disease-resistant. Hardy to Zone 4. A vigorous, upright shrub, attaining 5–6 feet, 10 feet if trained on supports. Makes a good hedge; tolerates some shade. Of 'Mme. Hardy' David Austin wrote, "only a few others can approach it for the sheer perfection of its flowers." J. A. Hardy, its hybridizer, was in charge of the renowned Luxembourg Gardens in Paris and named this immortal rose for his wife.

'Celsiana', damask.

'Mme. Hardy', damask.

Albas

'**Celestial**', alba, 8.6, light pink, cultivated before 1848. (Also called 'Céleste'.)

Large, semidouble, cupped light-pink blooms with a boss of golden stamens; rich fragrance; once-blooming; bears red hips. Dull grayish-green foliage is very disease-resistant; few prickles. Hardy to Zone 3 or 4. Grows into a substantial shrub 5–6 feet tall and nearly as wide. Tolerates some shade. 'Celestial' is highly praised for its delicate, heavenly beauty and performs better in warm climates than most albas.

'**Félicité Parmentier**', alba, 8.7, light pink, introduced in or before 1834.

Small, very double quartered blooms of soft flesh pink open flat, then reflex; deliciously fragrant; once-blooming. Foliage is gray-green; numerous dark prickles contrast with light-green stems and leaflets; very disease-resistant. Hardy to Zone 3 or 4. Forms a vigorous shrub of 4–5 feet in height and width. Tolerates partial shade. A good hedge rose and good for cutting.

'Félicité Parmentier', alba.

'**Mme. Plantier**', alba, 8.6, white, Plantier, 1835.

Medium-size creamy white, very double flat blooms, changing to pure white, with a green eye in the center, flowering generously in clusters; fragrant. Once-blooming, with a long flowering season. Good for cutting. Has glossy, small grayish-green foliage; very disease-resistant. Canes are virtually thornless. Hardy to Zone 3 or 4. Vigorous, bushy, spreading shrub of 4–6 feet in height and width; will

'Mme. Plantier', alba.

grow taller (10–12 feet or more) if trained onto a trellis or other support. Tolerates some shade.

Despite its official classification as a hybrid alba—believed to be a cross between *Rosa × alba* and *R. moschata*, the musk rose—some experts consider 'Mme. Plantier' a hybrid Noisette. Although it has the hardiness you'd expect from an alba, it grows well in climates as warm as Zone 8; some consider it the best alba for Southern gardens.

'Semi-plena', alba, 9.0, white, cultivated before 1867. (A sport of 'Maxima'. Also called 'The White Rose of York'.)

Large, semidouble milk-white blooms of 8–12 petals, with showy golden stamens; exquisitely fragrant; once-blooming; produces a good crop of large red hips in fall. Foliage is grayish green and very disease-resistant. Long prickles. Hardy to Zone 3 or 4. Forms a large, spreading shrub 5–7 feet in height and equal or greater width. Tolerates some shade. This sweet-smelling rose has been cultivated for the production of attar (fragrant essential oil) of roses.

'Semi-plena', alba.

Mosses

'Communis', moss, 8.3, medium pink, appeared in southern France about 1696. (Also called 'Common Moss', 'Centifolia Muscosa', 'Old Pink Moss', 'Mousseau Ancien', and 'Pink Moss'.)

Medium-size, mossy buds open into very double globular rich pink blooms; strong fragrance; once-blooming but with a long flowering period. Good for cutting. Foliage is dark green and coarsely toothed. Moderately disease-resistant.

'Communis', moss.

Hardy to Zone 4. Growth is spindly, reaching 4–7 feet in height. Very prickly. Considered the original and probably the best moss rose, 'Communis' is well-clad in the pine-scented growth that gives this class of rose its name.

'**Henri Martin**', moss, 8.8, medium red, Laffay, 1863. (Also called 'Red Moss'.)

Long, sparsely mossed buds open into medium-size globular, semidouble crimson blooms appearing in clusters; fragrant; once-blooming but generous in flowering. Produces orange-red hips. Lush foliage is medium green and moderately disease-resistant. Hardy to Zone 4 or 5. An upright, somewhat lax shrub reaching 5–6 feet in height. A profuse bloomer, 'Henri Martin' tolerates hot summers better than many old European roses. Makes a good hedge.

'Henri Martin', moss.

MORE GOOD SPECIES ROSES

R. banksiae banksiae (White Lady Banks), 9.5, white

R. banksiae 'Lutea' (Yellow Lady Banks), 9.1, light yellow

R. carolina (pasture rose), 8.1, medium pink

R. chinensis 'Viridiflora' (officially known as 'Green Rose' and classed as a China), 7.3, green

R. eglanteria (sweetbrier rose), 8.4, light pink

R. glauca (also known as *R. rubrifolia*), 8.8, medium pink

R. hugonis ('Father Hugo's Rose'), 8.5, medium yellow

R. laevigata (Cherokee rose), 8.6, white

R. laxa, not rated, white

R. moyesii, not rated, medium red

R. multiflora 'Carnea', not rated, light pink

R. palustris (swamp rose), not rated, medium pink

R. pomifera (apple rose), 6.3, medium pink

R. primula (incense rose), not rated, light yellow

R. roxburghii (chestnut rose), 8.7, medium pink

R. rugosa alboplena, not rated, white

R. sericea, not rated, white

R. setigera (prairie rose), 9.2, deep pink

R. spinosissima (Scotch or burnet rose; also known as *R. pimpinellifolia*), 8.4, white

R. virginiana, 8.6, medium pink

R. wichuraiana (memorial rose), 7.0, white

MORE GOOD ONCE-BLOOMING OLD ROSES

'Apothecary's Rose', gallica, 8.7, deep pink

'Belle Isis', gallica, 7.4, light pink

'Complicata', gallica, 8.9, pink blend

'Duc de Guiche', gallica, 7.6, mauve

'Duchesse de Montebello', gallica, not rated, light pink

'Hippolyte', gallica, not rated, mauve

'James Mason', gallica, not rated, medium red

'OEillet Flamand', gallica, not rated, pink blend

'Président de Sèze', gallica, 6.9, mauve

'Gloire de Guilan', damask, 6.5, light pink

'Ispahan', damask, 8.4, medium pink

'Kazanlik', damask, 7.6, deep pink

'Mme. Zöetmans', damask, 8.8, white

'St. Nicholas', damask, 7.7, deep pink

'York and Lancaster', damask, 7.6, pink blend

'Amélia', alba, not rated, medium pink

'Belle Amour', alba, 7.9, light pink

'Chloris', alba, not rated, light pink

'Great Maiden's Blush', alba, 9.1, white

'Jeanne d'Arc', alba, not rated, white

'Königin von Dänemark', alba, 8.6, medium pink

'Mme. Legras de St. Germain', alba, 7.9, white

'Maiden's Blush', alba, 7.9, white

'Maxima', alba, 8.4, white

'Fantin-Latour', centifolia, 8.5, light pink

'Petite de Hollande', centifolia, 7.5, medium pink

'Rose de Meaux', centifolia, 7.2, medium pink

'The Bishop', centifolia, 6.6, mauve

'Tour de Malakoff', centifolia, 7.1, mauve

'Capitaine John Ingram', moss, not rated, mauve

'Nuits de Young', moss, 7.2, dark red

'Perpetual White Moss', moss, not rated, white

'Salet', moss, 8.1, medium pink

'White Bath', moss, 7.5, white

'William Lobb', moss, 8.1, mauve

Hardy Repeat-blooming Old Roses

Those who love the sumptuous look of old-rose flowers yet seek repeat bloom can find both in the Bourbons, Portlands, and hybrid perpetuals. Although their history is difficult to establish, the Portlands may be descended from a hybrid of the twice-blooming 'Autumn Damask' and the ancient gallica 'Apothecary's Rose', with a touch of China blood as well. The class was more or less given up when repeat-blooming China and tea roses became widely available. (See the following section for more information about China and tea roses.)

The Bourbons are generally believed to be the result of a natural cross between a repeat-blooming China rose and a damask that took place on Ile de Bourbon, now called Réunion, in the Indian Ocean. Tall, vigorous, and repeat-blooming, the Bourbons bear lovely, full, fragrant flowers.

The hybrid perpetuals—wildly popular from the mid- to late 1800s—descended from hybrids involving Bourbons, Portlands, and teas. Near the end of their heyday their large blooms began to resemble fuller versions of the high-centered hybrid teas, which soon supplanted hybrid perpetuals.

'Frau Karl Druschki', hybrid perpetual, 7.7, white, Lambert, 1901.
(Also called 'F. K. Druschki', 'Reine des Neiges', 'Snow Queen', 'White American Beauty', and 'Snedronningen'.)

Pointed buds with a pink tinge open into large, double, snow-white blooms; center is sometimes touched with blush pink. Reliable repeat. Soft light-green foliage is susceptible to powdery mildew but more blackspot-resistant than that of many in its class. Quite prickly. Hardy to Zone 4 or 5. Vigorous, upright growth, reaching 5–7 feet in height. Its long stems and elegant blooms make it excellent for cutting. 'Frau Karl Druschki' tolerates Southern heat better than many hybrid perpetuals. Wherever it's grown, it requires good cultivation to keep disease to a minimum. A climbing sport was introduced in 1906.

'Frau Karl Druschki', hybrid perpetual.

'**Mme. Isaac Pereire**', Bourbon, 8.4, deep pink, Garçon, 1881.

Large, full, quartered blooms of deep rose-pink with shades of purple; intensely fragrant, with hints of raspberry; remontant. Hardy to Zone 5. Large dark-green foliage; moderately resistant to powdery mildew but susceptible to blackspot. Upright, leggy growth of 6–8 feet. 'Mme. Isaac Pereire' requires excellent soil, plenty of sun, and good air circulation to stay healthy. This gorgeous rose is worth the trou-

'Mme. Isaac Pereire', Bourbon.

ble, however, and has been praised by Graham Stuart Thomas as "possibly the most powerfully fragrant of all roses." Because it has long canes, it's a good choice for pegging—that is, pinning the tips of its branches to the ground, which strongly stimulates flowering all along the stems.

'**Rose de Rescht**', damask (some consider it a Portland), 8.9, deep pink, introduced to England from Persia or France in the 1940s.

Small, very full, deep fuchsia-red double blooms take on lilac hues as they fade; very fragrant; remontant. Well-clad in large dark-green semiglossy leaflets; disease-resistant. Moderately prickly. Hardy to Zone 4. Shrub is vigorous but compact, reaching about 3 feet. 'Rose de Rescht' will tolerate some shade and makes a good short hedge.

'**Stanwell Perpetual**', hybrid spinosissima, 8.5, white, Lee, 1838.

Medium-size flat, double, quartered blush-colored flowers that fade to white; sweet fragrance. Repeat-blooming, once established, putting on the biggest show in mid-summer. Foliage is small and grayish green; good disease-resistance. Very prickly canes. Hardy to Zone 3 or 4. A gracefully arching,

'Stanwell Perpetual', hybrid spinosissima.

suckering, twiggy shrub, reaching 4–5 feet in height and width. Makes a dense hedge. This variety's coarsely toothed leaflets often display a characteristic mottled purplish discoloration. Apparently a natural hybrid between *Rosa spinosissima* (the Scotch rose or burnet rose) and a damask, 'Stanwell Perpetual' is renowned for its long bloom season and ease of care. It is the only reliably repeating member of its class.

<table>
<tr><th colspan="1">MORE GOOD REPEAT-BLOOMING OLD ROSES</th></tr>
</table>

'Boule de Neige', Bourbon, 7.9, white
'Honorine de Brabant', Bourbon, 8.3, pink blend
'Zéphirine Drouhin', Bourbon, 8.1, medium pink

'Comte de Chambord', Portland, 8.3, pink blend

'Alfred Colomb', hybrid perpetual, 6.2, deep pink
'Baron Girod de l'Ain', hybrid perpetual, 7.1, red blend
'Baronne Prévost', hybrid perpetual, 8.7, medium pink
'Paul Neyron', hybrid perpetual, 8.1, medium pink
'Ulrich Brunner Fils', hybrid perpetual, 7.9, deep pink

Tender Repeat-blooming Old Roses

Although gardeners in the hotter parts of the Deep South and Southwest may find it hard to grow prize old European roses, three classes of tender antique roses shine in warm climates: Chinas, teas, and Noisettes.

The China and tea rose classes emerged from four "stud" roses brought from China in the late 1700s and early 1800s: 'Old Blush' (also known as 'Parsons' Pink China'), 'Slater's Crimson China', 'Hume's Blush Tea-Scented China', and 'Parks' Yellow Tea-Scented China'. Long cultivated in the Orient ('Old Blush' is thought to date back a thousand years), these free-flowering roses are responsible for giving modern varieties the capacity for season-long repeat. When Western rose breeders got their hands on them, a rose revolution began.

At about the same time that the Portland and Bourbon roses emerged, a class of roses called Noisettes appeared. In Charleston, South Carolina, John Champneys crossed 'Old Blush' and *Rosa moschata*, the musk rose, and gave seeds to his friend Philippe Noisette. Noisette sowed the seeds and was rewarded with a rose later named 'Blush Noisette', which in 1814 he sent to his brother Louis, in Paris. Louis introduced it three years later and went on to develop other varieties.

The best old roses for the Deep South and other hot climates, most Chinas, teas, and Noisettes are hardy to Zone 7 (some to Zone 6). The Chinas and their relatives the teas have smooth, twiggy canes, few prickles, and smooth, small, pointed leaflets. Although many Chinas are rather dwarf in habit, teas—whose ancestry includes the immense species rose *R. gigantea*—inherited the capacity for larger flowers and longer canes. Most Noisettes are at their best when trained as climbers; nearly all have excellent fragrance.

Chinas

'**Archduke Charles**', China, 8.3, red blend, Laffay, before 1837.

A seedling of 'Old Blush'. Medium-size, informal, cupped double blooms open pink, with darker outer petals, and mature to crimson; fragrant. Good for cutting. Foliage is dark green and large; few prickles. Disease-resistant but may get powdery mildew in dry weather. Hardy to Zone 7. An upright, vase-shaped shrub of 3–5 feet in height; good for hedging. 'Archduke Charles' is a perfect example of the Chinas' tendency for blooms to darken, not fade, as they age.

'**Cramoisi Supérieur**', China, 8.6, medium red, Coquereau, 1832.
(Also called 'Agrippina' and 'Lady Brisbane'. A seedling of 'Slater's Crimson China'.)

Small, double, globular, cupped blooms of velvety crimson-red with a silvery reverse, produced in

'Cramoisi Supérieur', China.

clusters; freely repeat-blooming; light fragrance has hints of raspberry. Dark-green, glossy, small foliage; very disease-resistant. Hardy to Zone 7. A twiggy bush, growing to a height of 3–5 feet. Makes a good everblooming hedge. A climbing form was introduced in 1885.

'**Mutabilis**', China, 8.7, yellow blend, cultivated before 1894.
(Also called 'Tipo Ideale' and *Rosa chinensis mutabilis.*)

'*Mutabilis*', *China.*

Slender red, pointed buds open into small single flowers that begin buff yellow and mature to orange, red, and ultimately crimson; reliable repeat bloom. Foliage is bronzy when new; reddish prickles; disease-resistant but may be susceptible to rust. Hardy to Zone 6. A twiggy, upright shrub 4–7 feet tall and 3–5 feet wide. This rose's charm is largely due to its constant bloom—reminding some of a flight of butterflies—and the unique mix of flower colors present at one time.

'**Old Blush**', China, 8.7, medium pink, introduced to Sweden in 1752 and to England before 1759; grown in China for a thousand years or more.
(Also known as 'Common Monthly', 'Old Pink Daily', 'Common Blush China', 'Old Pink China', and 'Parsons' Pink China'.)

'*Old Blush*', *China.*

Small, semidouble blooms of light and medium pink with deeper pink veins, in loose sprays; slight sweet-pea fragrance; constantly in bloom; forms orange hips. Medium-green glossy foliage; few prickles. Hardy to Zone 6. A twiggy, upright, vigorous shrub of 3–6 feet; good for hedging. An informal rose, 'Old Blush' is ideal for the gardener who wants a long-blooming, low-maintenance bush. Although in wet climates it may suffer from blackspot,

'Old Blush' endures despite periodic defoliation and is often found growing untended in Southern cemeteries. One of the first roses to start flowering each year and the last to stop.

Teas

'**Duchesse de Brabant**', tea, 8.6, light pink, Bernède, 1857.

Cupped, double, medium-size blooms of soft rosy pink; fragrance has hints of raspberry; good repeat. Well-clad in medium-green glossy leaflets; relatively disease-resistant. Moderately prickly. Hardy to Zone 7. A vase-shaped, vigorous bush, reaching 4–6 feet in height and 3–4 feet in width.

This charming rose is perhaps best known as President Theodore Roosevelt's favorite buttonhole flower. A white sport, 'Mme. Joseph Schwartz', was introduced in 1880.

'**Lady Hillingdon**', tea, 7.7, yellow blend, Lowe & Shawyer, 1910.

Long, pointed buds open into large, semidouble flowers of a rich apricot yellow, fading to cream white; yellow stamens; good tea fragrance; reliably repeat-blooming. Good for cutting. Young foliage and new growth are plum-colored; leaflets mature to glossy dark green; moderately disease-resistant. Few prickles. Hardy to Zone 6. An upright shrub growing 4–6 feet tall. A more vigorous climbing sport was introduced in 1917.

'Lady Hillingdon', tea.

'**Marie van Houtte**', tea, 7.5, pink blend, Ducher, 1871.

Large, very double, high-centered creamy yellow blooms tinged with rose; tea fragrance;

'Marie van Houtte', tea.

repeat-blooming. Leathery foliage of rich, glossy green; quite disease-resistant. Hardy to Zone 7. A sprawling, vigorous, free-flowering shrub reaching 4–6 feet in height.

'**Mrs. B. R. Cant**', tea, 8.7, medium pink, Cant, 1901.

Large, very full, double blooms of silvery rose with a deep rose reverse and buff-colored base; very fragrant; reliably repeat-blooming. Medium-green leathery foliage; disease-resistant. Hardy to Zone 7. Forms a large bush 6–8 feet tall and 5–7 feet wide. Good for cutting. A vigorous, generously flowering cultivar, 'Mrs. B. R. Cant' is considered one of the best roses for the Deep South.

'Mrs. B. R. Cant', tea.

Noisettes

'**Blush Noisette**', Noisette, 8.4, white, Noisette, 1817. (A seedling of 'Champneys' Pink Cluster'.)

Small pinkish-white cupped, semidouble flowers with yellow stamens, produced in clusters; rich musky fragrance; reliably repeat-blooming. Well-clad in light-green glossy foliage; disease-resistant. Few prickles. Hardy to Zone 6. A vigorous, sprawling shrub reaching 4–6 feet without support; grows to 10 feet or more if trained as a climber. 'Blush Noisette' was the first of its class.

'**Mme. Alfred Carrière**', Noisette, 9.0, white, Schwartz, 1879.

'Blush Noisette', Noisette.

Medium-size full, globular blooms of pale pinkish white fading to cream, borne in clusters; tea-rose fragrance; reliably repeat-blooming. Good for cutting. Medium-green semiglossy foliage; moderately disease-resistant. Fairly prickly. Hardy to Zone 6. A vigorous rose that can be grown as a very large arching shrub (10 feet in height and spread) or a climber, reaching heights of 18–20 feet with support. 'Mme. Alfred Carrière' requires plenty of sun and good air circulation to stay healthy.

'Rêve d'Or', Noisette, 9.4, medium yellow, Ducher, 1869.
(A seedling of 'Mme. Schultz'.)

Medium-size, double buff-yellow flowers with hints of salmon and peach; dark stamens; light, sweet fragrance; repeat-blooming. Good for cutting. Glossy rich green foliage; disease-resistant. Hardy to Zone 6. A vigorous climber, producing canes 10–15 feet in height.

'Rêve d'Or', Noisette.

MORE GOOD CHINAS, TEAS, AND NOISETTES

'Comtesse du Caÿla', China, 6.3, orange blend
'Ducher', China, 8.1, white
'Irène Watts', China, not rated, white
'Jean Bach Sisley', China, not rated, pink blend
'Rouletii', China, 7.6, medium pink
'Vincent Godsiff', China, not rated, medium red

'Adam', tea, not rated, medium pink
'Baronne Henriette de Snoy', tea, not rated, pink blend
'Bon Silène', tea, 4.9, deep pink
'Francis Dubreuil', tea, not rated, dark red
'Maman Cochet', tea, 7.6, pink blend

'Monsieur Tillier', tea, 8.0, orange-pink
'Perle des Jardins', tea, 7.4, light yellow
'Safrano', tea, 6.3, apricot blend

'Alister Stella Gray', Noisette, 7.5, light yellow
'Bougainville', Noisette, not rated, pink blend
'Céline Forestier', Noisette, 8.9, light yellow
'Jaune Desprez', Noisette, not rated, yellow blend
'Lamarque', Noisette, 8.9, white
'Maréchal Niel', Noisette, 7.4, medium yellow

Modern Roses

As the everblooming Chinas and teas entered hybridizers' breeding programs, the hybrid perpetuals they mixed with gave way to hybrid teas. Officially speaking, the first of this new class was 'La France', a tea–hybrid perpetual cross introduced in 1867, although some rosarians offer compelling arguments that earlier introductions were equally qualified to be considered hybrid teas. In any case, the class wasn't recognized as distinct from hybrid perpetuals until the 1880s.

'La France', officially considered the first hybrid tea.

The vivid hybrid foetida 'Soleil d'Or' brought warm colors into the hybrid tea class.

The most popular roses sold today, hybrid teas (and their descendants, the floribundas and grandifloras) are renowned for their bright colors and beautiful shapes. When you want a large, long-stemmed beauty to cut for a bouquet or enjoy in the garden, a hybrid tea is the natural choice. Exhibitors love these roses' urn-shaped buds and elegant flowers—and many hybrid teas are exceptionally fragrant as well, despite the often-heard claim that most modern roses are devoid of scent.

We can thank French hybridizer Joseph Pernet-Ducher for the deep yellows, vermilions, and bicolors now common among hybrid teas—as well as a few less-desirable traits. In 1900 he introduced 'Soleil d'Or', an orange-yellow cross between the red hybrid perpetual 'Antoine Ducher' and *Rosa foetida* 'Persiana', a golden-yellow species variant native to Iran. The latter contributed the genes for warm colors as well as winter dieback and proneness to blackspot—a fungal pest to which a species rose from the dry Middle East had no reason to develop resistance. Originally known as Pernetianas, Pernet-Ducher's roses were gradually merged into the hybrid tea class. Contemporary breeders have done much to undo the damage caused by *R. foetida* 'Persiana', while keeping its brilliant color heritage.

Polyanthas, the forerunners of floribundas, are diminutive, twiggy shrubs that continuously produce clusters of small, delicate blooms. The first polyantha, 'Pâquerette', was introduced in 1875, and its ancestry includes both multiflora and China genes. Teas were added to the mix and lent their characteristics to well-known cultivars such as 'Cécile Brünner' (1881) and 'Perle d'Or' (1884). (Polyanthas have been grouped with miniatures in the plant portraits that follow because of their common dwarf habit.)

Floribundas and grandifloras flower in clusters rather than one bloom to a stem as hybrid teas (ideally) do. The floribundas arose when Danish hybridizer D. T. Poulsen, in an effort to combine hardiness and beauty, crossed a polyantha and a hybrid tea. Sister seedlings 'Else Poulsen' and 'Kirsten Poulsen' were introduced in 1924 as hybrid polyanthas. The class name was coined by the American rose firm Jackson & Perkins in 1939. Whatever they're called, floribundas are often hardier and more disease-resistant than their hybrid tea cousins. Most put on an excellent show in the landscape, and many are suitable for low hedges.

The grandiflora class was introduced along with the beautiful and hard-working rose 'Queen Elizabeth' in 1954. Ironically, British rosarians don't recognize the class grandiflora, preferring to consider its members floribundas or hybrid teas. Grandifloras are often taller than both hybrid teas and floribundas, and their lengthy stems make them excellent producers of cut flowers. Their hardiness is comparable with that of hybrid teas.

Miniatures—the smallest of roses—now account for more than half of the new rose introductions each year. Although all minis descend from a single rose—the dwarf China now called 'Rouletii'—they have been and continue to be crossed with roses of many other classes. 'Rouletii' was discovered in Switzerland in 1918, and the class was born when the hybridizers J. W. de Vink of Holland and Pedro Dot of Spain began breeding it to larger roses.

Miniatures are short in stature, naturally, but their blooms, canes, and leaves should also be proportionately small. They make good candidates for container gardening and border edgings, and the larger minis can be used as landscape shrubs. Most are relatively hardy.

This is a class in which hybridizers in the United States shine: most of the better contemporary minis have been American-bred. As David Austin comments, "It is an odd fact that the miniatures have received more attention in the land of the 'bigger and better'—the United States of America—than anywhere else."

Hybrid Teas

'**Elina**', hybrid tea, 8.9, light yellow, Dickson, 1983. (Code name 'DICjana'; also called 'Peaudouce'.)

'Elina', hybrid tea.

Large, double, high-centered clear light-yellow to ivory blooms; slight fragrance. Good repeat and extremely profuse bloom. Well-clad in large, glossy, dark-green foliage. Generally disease-resistant but in some climates may be susceptible to powdery mildew. Moderately prickly. Hardy to Zone 6. A vigorous, tall bush, growing 5–6 feet in height. 'Elina' has won two gold medals and honors in Germany's ADR trials (1987). A popular U.S. exhibition rose for many years, it is also an easy-care hybrid tea—some feel the best yellow garden rose of its class. The name 'Peaudouce', as 'Elina' is called in Europe, is that of a brand of disposable diapers popular in the United Kingdom. Roses have been named to honor throat lozenges ('Fisherman's Friend'), perfume ('Evelyn'), an automobile ('Chrysler Imperial'), and even antiballistic missiles ('Scudbuster'), but this is no doubt a first.

'**Folklore**', hybrid tea, 8.5, orange blend, Kordes, 1977. (Code name 'KORlore'.)

Long, pointed buds open into large, double, high-centered soft-orange flowers with a lighter reverse. Reliable if somewhat slow repeat. Strong fragrance. Glossy, medium-green, disease-resistant foliage. Quite prickly. Hardy to Zone 5. Very tall and vigorous, reaching 6–8 feet. A high-ranking exhibition rose, 'Folklore' is also an easy garden-variety hybrid tea. One parent is the highly scented 'Fragrant Cloud'.

'Folklore', hybrid tea.

'**Kardinal**', hybrid tea, 8.9, medium red, Kordes, 1986. (Code name 'KORlingo'.)

Medium-size, high-centered, double medium-red flowers; slight fragrance. Reliable repeat; generous in bloom. Dark-green, disease-resistant, semi-glossy foliage. Hardy to Zone 6. Upright habit, growing 4–5 feet tall. Makes an excellent cut flower. Ohio rosarian Peter Schneider has called 'Kardinal' "perhaps the healthiest of all red hybrid teas."

'**Olympiad**', hybrid tea, 9.0, medium red, McGredy, 1982. (Code name 'MACauck'; also known as 'Olympia' and 'Olympiade'.)

Medium-size brilliant-red, velvety, double, high-centered blooms; slight fragrance. Reliable repeat; profuse bloom. Good for cutting. Foliage is large, medium green, and disease-resistant. Hardy to Zone 6. Upright, bushy habit, reaching a height of 4–5 feet. 'Olympiad', the official rose of the 1984 Summer

'Olympiad', hybrid tea.

Olympics, is one of the best red hybrid teas ever. Rosarians praise its brilliant nonfading color, vigor, and long stems, and its hybridizer, Sam

McGredy of New Zealand, says it has earned more money than any of his other introductions. 'Olympiad' was named an AARS winner in 1984 and received a gold medal the following year in Portland, Oregon.

'**Pascali**', hybrid tea, 8.1, white, Lens, 1963.
(Code name 'LENip'; also called 'Blanche Pascal'.)

'Pascali', hybrid tea.

Medium-size, creamy white, double, high-centered blooms. Reliable repeat. Good for cutting. Dark-green disease-resistant foliage. Moderately prickly. Hardy to Zone 6. Vigorous growth to around 4 feet in height. 'Pascali' has taken numerous honors: two gold medals, an AARS award (1969), and the designation World's Favorite Rose (1991). Widely regarded as the best white hybrid tea, it inherited disease-resistance from parent 'Queen Elizabeth' and makes an excellent cut flower. A climbing sport was introduced in 1978.

'**Pristine**', hybrid tea, 9.1, white, Warriner, 1978.
(Code name 'JACpico'.)

Large, double, high-centered near-white flowers with a light-pink tinge; slight fragrance. Reliable and rapid repeat bloom. Large dark-green foliage is resistant to powdery mildew. Quite prickly. Hardy to Zone 7 or 8. Upright growth habit, reaching a height of 4–5 feet. 'Pristine' makes an excellent cut flower, bearing very substantial blooms. A top exhibition rose in the United States, it was Jackson & Perkins' Rose of the Year in 1978 and the following year won a gold medal in Portland, Oregon. Although it also won England's Edland Fragrance Medal, it is less fragrant in America.

'**Silver Jubilee**', hybrid tea, 9.4, pink blend, Cocker, 1978.

Large, high-centered, double blooms of silvery pink and coral-orange with a darker reverse; light fragrance. Reliable repeat; very free-flowering. Good for cutting. Well-clad in fine, glossy medium-green disease-resistant foliage. Hardy to Zone 6. Vigorous and upright, growing 3–4 feet tall. British rosarian Peter Beales called 'Silver Jubilee' "one of the best roses ever raised," and its high ARS rating reflects its reliability, robust good health, and top-notch exhibition form. It was named to commemorate the twenty-fifth anniversary of Queen Elizabeth II's coronation. In 1977 it won the British Royal National Rose Society's President's International Trophy and in 1980 and 1981 was awarded gold medals in Belfast, Northern Ireland, and Portland, Oregon. 'Parkdirektor Riggers', a hardy korde-sii shrub (and an ADR winner) introduced in 1957, figures in its ancestry.

'Silver Jubilee', hybrid tea.

Floribundas

'**Dicky**', floribunda, 8.8, orange pink, Dickson, 1983.

(Code name 'DICkimono'; also called 'Anisley Dickson' and 'Münchner Kindl'.)

Large double blooms of reddish salmon-pink with a lighter reverse, borne in clusters; slight fragrance. Very good repeat. Foliage is medium green, glossy, and disease-resistant. Few prickles. Hardy to Zone 5. An upright, bushy plant, growing 3–3$^{1}/_{2}$ feet tall. A popular exhibition floribunda in the 1980s and 1990s, 'Dicky' is

'Dicky', floribunda.

widely praised for its excellent color, vigor, health, and profusion of bloom. In 1984 it received the Royal National Rose Society's President's International Trophy.

'Escapade', floribunda, 8.7, mauve, Harkness, 1967.
(Code name 'HARpade'.)

Large, semidouble magenta-rose blooms with white centers, borne in large clusters; fragrant. Good repeat; flowers profusely. Good for cutting. Foliage is a glossy, disease-resistant light green. Hardy to Zone 5. Forms an upright, branching bush about 3 feet tall. An easy-to-please garden variety as well as a top exhibition rose, 'Escapade' is the result of a cross between the grandiflora 'Pink Parfait' and the grape-purple polyantha 'Baby Faurax'. It won gold medals in Belfast, Northern Ireland, and Baden-Baden, Germany, in 1969 and an ADR award in 1973.

'Hannah Gordon', floribunda, 8.9, pink blend, Kordes, 1983.
(Code name 'KORweiso'; also called 'Raspberry Ice'.)

'Hannah Gordon', floribunda.

Large, double white blooms with cherry-pink edges, carried in large clusters; slight fragrance. Reliable repeat; blooms consistently. Foliage is large, medium green, semiglossy, and disease-resistant. Quite prickly. Hardy to Zone 5. Bushy, upright growth, reaching a height of 4–6 feet. Another healthy offering from the Kordes family, 'Hannah Gordon' is deservedly praised for its wonderful color and flower form. It makes a fine hedge.

'Livin' Easy', floribunda, not rated, orange blend, Harkness, 1992.
(Code name 'HARwelcome'; also called 'Fellowship'.)

Medium-size, full, ruffled apricot blossoms, aging orange, borne in large clusters. Reliable repeat; fruity fragrance. Well-clad in large, dark-green, glossy foliage; very good blackspot resistance. Hardy to Zone 5. Branching, medium growth, to about 3 feet. This undemanding floribunda won a gold medal from the Royal National Rose Society in 1990 and an AARS award in 1996.

'**Playboy**', floribunda, 8.1, red blend, Cocker, 1976.

Large, single scarlet-and-orange flowers with golden eye and showy stamens; slight fragrance. Reliable repeat. Dark-green glossy foliage has moderate disease-resistance. Fairly prickly. Hardy to Zone 5 or 6. Forms a compact, bushy shrub about 3 feet tall. 'Playboy' is renowned for its eye-catching, brilliant blooms. In 1989 it won a gold medal in Portland, Oregon.

'**Sexy Rexy**', floribunda, 9.0, medium pink, McGredy, 1984.
(Code name 'MACrexy'; also called 'Heckenzauber' and 'Sexy Hexy'.)

'*Sexy Rexy*', *floribunda*.

Medium-size double blooms of medium to light pink, borne in large sprays. Profuse bloom and reliable, if somewhat slow, repeat. Small dark-green glossy foliage has good resistance to powdery mildew. Quite thorny. Hardy to Zone 5. Upright, bushy growth, reaching 3–4 feet in height. One of Sam McGredy's most popular roses, 'Sexy Rexy' makes a fine cut flower and a good landscape plant, although it must be deadheaded to ensure good repeat. It's been awarded four gold medals in Scotland, New Zealand, and the United States.

'**Showbiz**', floribunda, 8.6, medium red, Tantau, 1981.
(Code name 'TANweieke'; also called 'Bernhard Däneke' and 'Ingrid Weibull'.)

'*Showbiz*', *floribunda*.

Medium-size double intense-scarlet flowers with a hint of orange, blooming in large sprays. Reliable and rapid repeat. Dark, disease-resistant semiglossy foliage. Hardy to Zone 5. Compact, bushy growth to around 3 feet. Constantly in bloom, 'Showbiz' makes a terrific visual impact in the landscape. It won an AARS award in 1985.

'Sunsprite', floribunda, 8.7, deep yellow, Kordes, 1977.
(Code name 'KORresia'; also known as 'Friesia' and
    'Sun Sprite'.)

Large double deep-yellow flowers with strong
fragrance that's been likened to cinnamon toast.
Medium-green, glossy, disease-resistant foliage.
Moderately prickly. Hardy to Zone 5. Sturdy,
bushy growth, reaching a height of about 3 feet.
Perhaps the best yellow floribunda, 'Sunsprite'
is one of only a handful of roses to win the ARS   'Sunsprite', floribunda.
James Alexander Gamble Rose Fragrance Award
(1979). It also received a gold medal in Baden-Baden, Germany, in 1972.

Grandifloras

'Aquarius', grandiflora, 7.7, pink blend, Armstrong, 1971.
(Code name 'ARMaq'.)

Large, double high-centered pink-and-cream blooms; slight fragrance.
Foliage is large, leathery, and medium-green. Good disease-resistance.
Hardy to Zone 5. A vigorous, bushy shrub that reaches 4–5 feet in height.
The 1970 winner of a gold medal in Geneva, 'Aquarius' received an AARS
award the following year. It makes a good cut flower.

'Queen Elizabeth', grandiflora, 7.4, medium pink,
    Lammerts, 1954.
(Also called 'Queen of England' and 'The Queen
    Elizabeth Rose'.)

Large, medium-pink, loosely informal, cupped,
double flowers, blooming singly and in clusters;
fragrant. Reliable repeat bloom. Good for cutting. Dark-green, leathery, disease-resistant
foliage. Fairly prickly. Hardy to Zone 6. Very   'Queen Elizabeth', grandiflora.

vigorous, forming an upright bush 5–7 feet tall. The grandiflora class was created for this rose, still widely considered the best of its kind. An easy beginner's rose, 'Queen Elizabeth' has many honors to its credit, including the AARS designation, the Royal National Rose Society President's International Trophy, the ARS National Gold Medal Certificate for Outstanding Performance, and World's Favorite Rose. A climbing form was introduced in 1957.

'**Tournament of Roses**', grandiflora, 8.0, medium pink, Warriner, 1988.
(Code name 'JACient'; also called 'Berkeley' and 'Poesie'.)

Large, double, high-centered blooms of light coral-pink with a deeper-pink reverse, borne singly or in clusters. Good repeat; prolific bloom. Large dark-green foliage is semiglossy and moderately disease-resistant. Large prickles. Hardy to Zone 7. Upright and bushy, growing 3–5 feet tall. This cultivar's color and foliage were very highly rated in the ARS's annual Proof of the Pudding assessment of new roses (now called Roses in Review) in 1989. 'Tournament of Roses' won an AARS award the same year.

'Tournament of Roses', grandiflora.

Polyanthas

'**Cécile Brünner**', polyantha, 8.2, light pink, Ducher, 1881.

Small, double soft-pink flowers in clusters; constantly in bloom; slight fragrance. Sparse, small dark-green semiglossy foliage. Disease-resistant; if foliage is affected, the plant suffers little or no loss of vigor. Hardy to Zone 5. Twiggy, dwarf, upright growth to 3–4 feet; few prickles. 'Cécile Brünner' performs well in both cold and hot climates. A very good climbing form was introduced in 1894. (Illustration on page 74.)

'Alec's Red', hybrid tea, 7.5, medium red

'Artistry', hybrid tea, not rated, orange blend, AARS

'Audrey Hepburn', hybrid tea, 7.7 interim rating, light pink

'Belami', hybrid tea, 7.3, orange-pink

'Bewitched', hybrid tea, 7.3, medium pink, AARS

'Brandy', hybrid tea, 7.0, apricot blend, AARS

'Bride's Dream', hybrid tea, 8.0, light pink

'Brigadoon', hybrid tea, 7.3, pink blend, AARS

'Chrysler Imperial', hybrid tea, 7.5, dark red, AARS

'Crystalline', hybrid tea, 8.4, white

'Double Delight', hybrid tea, 8.7, red blend, AARS

'Esther Geldenhuys', hybrid tea, 7.5, orange-pink

'First Prize', hybrid tea, 8.6, pink blend, AARS

'Fragrant Cloud', hybrid tea, 8.1, orange-red

'Honor', hybrid tea, 7.6, white, AARS

'Ingrid Bergman', hybrid tea, 7.1, dark red

'Jadis', hybrid tea, 7.1, medium pink

'Jardins de Bagatelle', hybrid tea, 7.5, white

'Just Joey', hybrid tea, 7.9, orange blend

'Lafter', hybrid tea, not rated, yellow blend

'Maid of Honour', hybrid tea, 7.3, yellow blend

'Marijke Koopman', hybrid tea, 9.0, medium pink

'Midas Touch', hybrid tea, 7.8, deep yellow, AARS

'Mon Cheri', hybrid tea, 6.9, red blend, AARS

'Opening Night', hybrid tea, not rated, dark red, AARS

'Paul Shirville', hybrid tea, 7.4, orange-pink

'Peace', hybrid tea, 8.4, yellow blend, AARS

'Perfect Moment', hybrid tea, 7.5, red blend, AARS

'Peter Frankenfeld', hybrid tea, 8.2, deep pink

'Polarstern', hybrid tea, 7.7, white

'Precious Platinum', hybrid tea, 7.3, medium red

'Secret', hybrid tea, 7.7, pink blend, AARS

'Sheer Elegance', hybrid tea, 7.7, orange-pink, AARS

'The McCartney Rose', hybrid tea, 8.3, medium pink

'Touch of Class', hybrid tea, 9.3, orange-pink, AARS

'Uncle Joe', hybrid tea, 8.1, dark red

'White Masterpiece', hybrid tea, 7.5, white

'Yves Piaget', hybrid tea, 7.5, deep pink

'Anabell', floribunda, 8.0, orange blend

'Apricot Nectar', floribunda, 8.0, apricot blend, AARS

'Betty Prior', floribunda, 8.2, medium pink

'Bill Warriner', floribunda, not rated, orange-pink

'Brass Band', floribunda, 7.9, apricot blend, AARS

'Cathedral', floribunda, 7.5, apricot blend, AARS

'Cherish', floribunda, 7.7, orange-pink, AARS

'Class Act', floribunda, 7.6, white, AARS

'Europeana', floribunda, 9.0, dark red, AARS

'First Edition', floribunda, 8.4, orange-pink, AARS

'Gene Boerner', floribunda, 8.5, medium pink, AARS

'Goldmarie', floribunda, 7.3, deep yellow

'Grüss an Aachen', floribunda, 8.3, light pink

'Iceberg', floribunda, 8.9, white

'Little Darling', floribunda, 8.3, yellow blend

'Margaret Merril', floribunda, 8.5, white

'Nearly Wild', floribunda, 7.4, medium pink

'Playgirl', floribunda, 8.1, medium pink

'Pleasure', floribunda, 7.9, medium pink, AARS

'Regensberg', floribunda, 8.2, pink blend

'Sea Pearl', floribunda, 7.4, pink blend

'Simplicity', floribunda, 8.0, medium pink

'Spartan', floribunda, 7.3, orange-red

'Sun Flare', floribunda, 8.3, medium yellow, AARS

'Trumpeter', floribunda, 8.0, orange-red

'Camelot', grandiflora, 7.2, orange-pink, AARS

'Gold Medal', grandiflora, 8.6, medium yellow

'Love', grandiflora, 7.0, red blend, AARS

'Pearlie Mae', grandiflora, not rated, apricot blend

'Pink Parfait', grandiflora, 8.1, pink blend, AARS

'Shreveport', grandiflora, 6.5, orange blend, AARS

'**Marie Pavié**', polyantha, 8.8, white, Alégatière, 1888. (Also called 'Marie Pavic' and 'Marie Paviér'.)

Medium-size, flat, double white flowers with flesh-tinted centers, carried in clusters. Musk fragrance. Reliable repeat; very free-blooming. Large dark-green foliage is disease-resistant. Nearly thornless. Hardy to Zone 5. Vigorous, twiggy growth, reaching 2–4 feet in height. 'Marie Pavié' is ideal as an easy-care, everblooming dwarf landscape plant or low hedge.

'Cécile Brünner', polyantha

'**Perle d'Or**', polyantha, 8.3, yellow blend, Rambaux, 1884.
(Also called 'Yellow Cécile Brünner'.)

Small, dainty, double golden-pink flowers are borne in clusters; fragrant. Reliable repeat; constantly in bloom. Foliage is soft green and very disease-resistant. Hardy to Zone 6. Twiggy, upright growth reaching 3–4 feet in height. 'Perle d'Or' is a cross between an unnamed polyantha and the tea rose 'Mme. Falcot'. A charming rose with an iron constitution, 'Perle d'Or' is a good low-maintenance choice for beginners.

'Perle d'Or', polyantha.

'**The Fairy**', polyantha, 8.7, light pink, Bentall, 1932.

Small, cupped, double pink blooms in clusters along the entire length of canes. Flowering begins somewhat late in the season but continues unabated till fall. Flowers will fade in hot sun, so consider a site with afternoon shade if you garden in a hot climate. Well-clad in tiny medium-green, glossy foliage. Very disease-resistant. Prickly canes. Hardy to Zone 4. Low,

'The Fairy', polyantha.

spreading shrub reaches 2–3 feet in height and 3–4 feet in width. Its name notwithstanding, 'The Fairy' is nearly indestructible.

'White Pet', polyantha, 8.5, white, Henderson, 1879.
(Also called 'Little White Pet'.)

Small, pompon-shaped, double white blooms in large clusters. Light fragrance; constantly in bloom. Abundant dark-green foliage is very disease-resistant. Hardy to Zone 5. Dwarf, mounding growth, reaching about 2 feet in height and width. Another dauntless polyantha.

Miniatures

'Gourmet Popcorn', miniature, 8.7, white, Desamero, 1986.
(Code name 'WEOpop'; also called 'Summer Snow'.)

Medium-size, pure-white, flat, semidouble flowers with yellow stamens, in large sprays; blooms abundantly. Slight honey fragrance. Large dark-green foliage; good disease-resistance. Hardy to Zone 5. Rounded and bushy, reaching 18–30 inches in height. An exceptional garden rose, 'Gourmet Popcorn' also performs well in containers and hanging baskets. It is a sport of 'Popcorn'.

'Jean Kenneally', miniature, 9.5, apricot blend, Bennett, 1984.
(Code name 'TINeally'.)

Medium-size, hybrid tea–form, double pale- to medium-apricot blooms; slight fragrance; continuous bloom. Foliage is medium green and semiglossy. Needs protection where powdery mildew is a problem. Hardy to Zone 5. Upright bushy habit, reaching a height of 2–3 feet. Color fades somewhat in hot weather; consider a site with some afternoon shade. One of the

'Jean Kenneally', miniature.

best minis ever, 'Jean Kenneally' received the ARS Award of Excellence in 1986. Its large blooms (for a mini) are good for cutting.

'**Little Artist**', miniature, 8.8, red blend, McGredy, 1982. (Code names 'MACmanly' and 'MACmanley'; also called 'Top Gear'.)

'Little Artist', miniature.

Medium-size semidouble blooms with off-white base and reverse, "hand-painted" in red; showy stamens. Fragrant, with steady flower production. Small medium-green foliage is semiglossy and disease-resistant. Hardy to Zone 5 or 6. Upright growth reaching 12–18 inches. 'Little Artist' is one of New Zealand hybridizer Sam McGredy's hand-painted series—so named because the blend of colors on each bloom looks individually applied.

'**Magic Carrousel**', miniature, 8.9, red blend, Moore, 1972. (Code names 'MORroussel' and 'MOORcar'.)

'Magic Carrousel', miniature.

Medium-size, high-centered, semidouble white blooms edged in red. Reliable repeat; generous in flowering. Slight fragrance. Good for cutting. Small medium-green, glossy, disease-resistant foliage. Hardy to Zone 5. Upright, bushy habit, reaching 18–24 inches. 'Magic Carrousel' won the ARS Award of Excellence in 1975 and is a favorite exhibition and garden variety.

'**Minnie Pearl**', miniature, 9.5, pink blend, Saville, 1982. (Code name 'SAVahowdy'.)

Small hybrid tea–form light-pink blooms with a darker reverse. Reliable repeat; prolific bloom. Slight fragrance; makes a good cut flower. Foliage is small, medium-green, and semiglossy, with good disease-resistance. Hardy to Zone 5. Habit is upright, reaching 18–24 inches. A fine garden variety as well as a long-standing show champion, 'Minnie Pearl' is praised for its lovely color and long stems. In the American Rose society's 1986 Proof of the Pudding assessment of new roses, 'Minnie Pearl'—named for the character played by much-loved Grand Ole Opry performer Sarah Cannon— was described as "the archetype of mini excellence."

'Rainbow's End', miniature, 9.0, yellow blend, Saville, 1984.
(Code name 'SAValife'.)

Medium-size, double, high-centered deep-yellow blooms; in full sun, red petal edges develop. Small dark-green, glossy foliage is disease-resistant. Hardy to Zone 5. Upright, bushy habit, growing to a height of 16–22 inches. A very easy plant with outstanding form and prolific bloom, 'Rainbow's End' received the ARS Award of Excellence in 1986. A climbing sport was introduced in 1998.

'Rainbow's End', miniature.

'Rise 'n' Shine', miniature, 8.8, medium yellow, Moore, 1977.
(Also called 'Golden Sunblaze' and 'Golden Meillandina'.)

Medium-size, double, high-centered, rich medium-yellow flowers; good for cutting and produced continuously. Light-green matte foliage is moderately disease-resistant. Hardy to Zone 5. Rounded, bushy growth reaches 12–20 inches. A climbing sport was released in 1990. 'Rise 'n' Shine'—perhaps the best yellow miniature—won the ARS Award of Excellence in 1978.

'**Starina**', miniature, 8.7, orange-red, Meilland, 1965. (Code names 'MEIgabi' and 'MEIgali'.)

Medium-size, double, high-centered orange-scarlet blooms with yellow-tinged base; good as a cut flower. Glossy dark-green, disease-resistant foliage. Hardy to Zone 5. Vigorous growth, reaching 12–18 inches. In 1968 the very popular 'Starina' won a gold medal in Japan; three years later it received ADR honors.

'Starina', miniature.

MORE GOOD POLYANTHAS AND MINIATURES

'Baby Faurax', polyantha, 7.5, mauve
'China Doll', polyantha, 8.2, medium pink
'Clotilde Soupert', polyantha, 7.3, white
'La Marne', polyantha, 8.8, pink blend
'Margo Koster', polyantha, 7.5, orange blend
'Mevrouw Nathalie Nypels', polyantha, 7.7, medium pink

'Beauty Secret', miniature, 8.2, medium red, ARS Award of Excellence
'Child's Play', miniature, 8.0, white, AARS, ARS Award of Excellence
'Cinderella', miniature, 8.2, white
'Debut', miniature, 7.4, red blend, AARS
'Judy Fischer', miniature, 7.4, medium pink, ARS Award of Excellence
'Marriotta', miniature, 7.0, deep pink
'Mary Marshall', miniature, 7.6, orange blend, ARS Award of Excellence
'Millie Walters', miniature, 8.7, orange-pink
'New Beginning', miniature, 7.1, orange blend, AARS
'Rose Gilardi', miniature, 7.1, red blend
'Rosy Dawn', miniature, 7.6, yellow blend
'Show 'n' Tell', miniature, 7.5, orange blend
'Winsome', miniature, 8.5, mauve, ARS Award of Excellence

Shrub Roses

Talk about a mixed bag: shrub roses include everything from hybrid rugosas, many of which were introduced as early as the late 1800s, and hybrid musks, a class created in 1913, to the latest in everblooming landscape roses. Many roses in this class inherited better-than-average disease-resistance from their rugosa, wichuraiana, multiflora, and other species ancestors.

Today's hybridizers recognize that many gardeners have little time to devote to fussy plants and would prefer to minimize or eliminate the use of chemical sprays. In the shrub category you'll find some of the most disease-resistant roses ever—ideal choices for organic gardeners or anyone looking for plants that combine high performance and low maintenance. Top choices include shrubs in the class kordesii, the Meidiland series created by the House of Meilland in France, the Explorer series from Agriculture Canada, and the winter-hardy shrubs bred by the late Griffith Buck.

Although Buck, a professor at Iowa State University, hybridized more than eighty-five cultivars, few are widely available. All are hardy—at least to Zone 5—and most are disease-resistant, in large part because of the Darwinian way Buck treated his seedlings. He didn't spray them with fungicides or provide any winter protection, so only those that could hold their foliage and survive the Iowa winters were candidates for introduction. His best-known and most readily available rose is the shrub 'Carefree Beauty', but a number of others are well worth mail-ordering from specialty rose catalogs.

A popular new series within the shrub group is composed of the English roses bred and introduced by David Austin of Albrighton, England. Austin's quest has been to combine the refined beauty and scent of old European roses with the repeat bloom of modern roses, and many of his more than one hundred introductions succeed beautifully. Not all are particularly disease-resistant—though no more problematic than the average hybrid tea—but most are lovely and fragrant.

Hybrid Rugosas

Forming one of the larger classes within the shrub group, hybrid rugosas are the result of crosses between species (and other hybrid) rugosas and cultivars from an amazing array of classes, including hybrid teas, floribundas, hybrid perpetuals, ramblers, polyanthas, and damasks. Many of the offspring combine the exceptional disease-resistance, hardiness, and fragrance of the rugosas with semidouble or double blooms, contributed by the other parent. Often hardy to Zone 3 or 4, these hybrids make perhaps the ideal low-maintenance landscape roses. Their characteristically wrinkled, or rugose, foliage reacts badly to spraying, but most cultivars remain healthy without it and tolerate disease if it occurs.

Rugosas can endure slightly drier conditions than most roses, as well as some shade, although flowering will be reduced. Many hybrids form orange to red hips in fall, and some have attractive fall color.

These hybrids are at their best in cool and moderate climates; many sulk in Zone 8 and hotter areas. More heat-tolerant cultivars include 'Sir Thomas Lipton', 'Conrad Ferdinand Meyer', 'Blanc Double de Coubert', 'Jens Munk', and 'Sarah Van Fleet'.

Hybrid Musks

These excellent shrubs, first introduced in 1913 by the Rev. Joseph Pemberton of Essex, England, have only a tenuous connection with the true musk rose (*Rosa moschata*). Their ancestry includes *R. multiflora*, Noisette, and tea, and from the Noisettes—descended from a cross between *R. moschata* and 'Old Blush'—they inherited their light, musky scent. More disease-resistant and shade-tolerant than many roses, the hybrid musks are easy-care and free-flowering, with small- to medium-size blooms borne in generous sprays. Most grow 4–6 feet tall and about as wide; a number can be trained as pillar roses or small climbers.

Kordesiis

The antecedent to this class is 'Max Graf', a hybrid rugosa (thought to be a cross between *R. rugosa* and *R. wichuraiana*) introduced in 1919. The cultivar ultimately reached the Kordes nursery in Sparrieshoop, Germany, where Wilhelm Kordes spent years trying to self-pollinate the not-very-fertile plant. In 1940 he succeeded, producing *R. × kordesii*. The class that arose from that hybrid species includes a number of large shrubs and climbers that combine excellent hardiness and disease-resistance.

Hybrid Rugosas

'**Agnes**', hybrid rugosa, 7.7, light yellow, Saunders, 1900.

Large, papery, pale amber double flowers; delicate fragrance. Profuse nonrecurrent bloom. Medium-green, very wrinkled foliage. Somewhat susceptible to blackspot (the legacy of its parent *Rosa foetida* 'Persiana') and rust. Many prickles. Hardy to Zone 3. Vigorous and bushy, growing 5–6 feet in height and about an equal width. Despite its single season of bloom and greater disease-proneness, 'Agnes' is the first and best yellow rugosa. It was introduced by Canada's Central Experimental Farm at Ottawa in 1922.

'Agnes', hybrid rugosa.

'**Blanc Double de Coubert**', hybrid rugosa, 8.7, white, Cochet-Cochet, 1892.

Medium-size, semidouble or loosely double silky white blooms; strong, spicy fragrance. Reliably repeat-blooming, usually till frost. Very rugose dark-green, disease-resistant foliage. Hardy to Zone 2 or 3. Vigorous, upright growth, reaching 5–6 feet. Tolerates some shade. One of this lovely rose's parents is the climbing tea 'Sombreuil', which seems to have conferred greater tolerance of Southern

'Blanc Double de Coubert', hybrid rugosa.

heat. The renowned English gardener Gertrude Jekyll praised 'Blanc Double de Coubert' as "one of the best of roses" for the purity of its white blossoms as well as its good repeat and polished foliage.

'**Hansa**', hybrid rugosa, 8.3, medium red, Schaum & Van Tol, 1905. (Also called 'Hansen's'.)

Large, double mauve-red blooms; strong clove fragrance. Reliable repeat in fall but little bloom between cycles. Sets many large orange-red hips if not deadheaded. Rich-green rugose foliage with good fall color. Very disease-resistant. Hardy to Zone 3. A vigorous, vase-shaped shrub, reaching 6–7 feet in height and width. Tolerates some shade. 'Hansa' is a good choice for hedging.

'**Henry Hudson**', hybrid rugosa, 9.1, white, Svejda, 1976.

Rounded pink buds open into medium-size, flat, semidouble informal white flowers with yellow stamens. Reliable repeat. Clove fragrance. Well-clad in medium-green rugose leaflets; very disease-resistant. Hardy to Zone 2 or 3. A low, bushy shrub, growing about 4 feet tall and 3 feet wide. Tolerates some shade. One of the Canadian Explorer series, 'Henry Hudson' makes a good short hedge.

'**Jens Munk**', hybrid rugosa, 9.2, medium pink, Svejda, 1974.

'Jens Munk', hybrid rugosa.

Medium-size, semidouble lilac-pink blooms with yellow stamens; some petals may be marked with a white streak. Continuously in bloom; light, spicy fragrance. Produces a small crop of hips if not deadheaded. Disease-resistant foliage is small, medium green, and rugose. Hardy to Zone 2 or 3. Forms a vigorous, upright shrub 4–5 feet tall. Can take some shade. 'Jens Munk', another in the Canadian Explorer series, tolerates Southern summers. Makes a good hedge.

'Roseraie de l'Haÿ', hybrid rugosa, 9.0, dark red, Cochet-Cochet, 1901.

Large, full, very fragrant, semidouble crimson blooms age to rosy magenta. Strong clove-and-cinnamon fragrance. Good repeat. Good dark-green, rugose foliage; quite disease-resistant. Hardy to Zone 4. A vigorous, spreading 7- to 9-foot shrub. Tolerates some shade. One of the most beautiful of its class, 'Roseraie de l'Haÿ' was named for the renowned French rose garden founded at l'Haÿ, near Paris, in 1893.

'Roseraie de l'Haÿ', hybrid rugosa.

A garden room at Roseraie du Val-de-Marne (formerly known as Roseraie de l'Haÿ), one of the world's finest rose gardens, outside Paris.

Hybrid Musks

'**Ballerina**', hybrid musk, 8.8, medium pink, Bentall, 1937.

'*Ballerina*', *hybrid musk.*

Small, single bright-pink flowers with a white eye and yellow stamens, borne in large clusters. Light sweet-pea fragrance. Very free-flowering, with reliable repeat. Foliage is light green and semiglossy, with good disease-resistance. Few prickles. Hardy to Zone 5 or 6. Vigorous arching growth, 3–5 feet tall and wide. Tolerates some shade. Makes a fine hedge. After Joseph Pemberton's death in 1926 Ann and J. A. Bentall continued producing hybrid musks. Ann bred 'Ballerina' and 'Buff Beauty', two of the best in the class, as well as the polyantha 'The Fairy'.

'**Buff Beauty**', hybrid musk, 8.1, apricot blend, Bentall, 1939.

'*Buff Beauty*', *hybrid musk.*

Medium-size, double apricot-yellow flowers in large clusters; tea-rose fragrance. Reliable repeat. Large, thick, medium-green semiglossy foliage with good disease-resistance; moderately prickly. Hardy to Zone 5 or 6. Vigorous spreading growth to 6 feet, with rather rigid laterally growing canes. Can be trained as a short climber or pillar rose, reaching 8 feet or more with support. Tolerates some shade. One of the best-known hybrid musks, 'Buff Beauty' is loved for its unusual buff-apricot blooms.

'**Cornelia**', hybrid musk, 9.0, pink blend, Pemberton, 1925.

Small, double flattish strawberry rosettes flushed yellow, with yellow stamens, borne in sprays. Sweet fragrance. Reliable repeat, with good late-season bloom. Dark-green, glossy, disease-resistant foliage. Moderately prickly. Hardy to Zone 5 or 6. Very vigorous, arching, lax growth, reaching 5–7 feet in height and an equal spread. Tolerates some shade. 'Cornelia' can be trained as a short climber and with support can reach 12 feet.

'Cornelia', hybrid musk.

'**Moonlight**', hybrid musk, 8.2, light yellow, Pemberton, 1913.

Small, semidouble lemony-white flowers with prominent yellow stamens, borne in clusters; good display of hips in fall. Musk-rose fragrance. Excellent repeat. Dark-green foliage is glossy and disease-resistant. Hardy to Zone 5 or 6. Forms a vigorous, lax, spreading shrub 5–6 feet tall or more. Tolerates some shade. Can be trained as a small climber, reaching 8–12 feet with support.

'**Vanity**', hybrid musk, 8.3, deep pink, Pemberton, 1920.

Dainty, near-single rose-pink blooms in large sprays; very fragrant. Reliable repeat. Sparse leathery foliage is dark green and very disease-resistant. Hardy to Zone 5 or 6. Vigorous spreading growth, reaching a height of about 6 feet and greater width. Tolerates some shade.

Kordesiis

'**Champlain**', kordesii, 8.8, dark red, Svejda, 1982.

Large, double dark-red blooms with slight fragrance. Constantly in bloom. Foliage is small, yellow-green, and disease-resistant. Very prickly. Hardy to

Zone 4. A compact shrub, reaching 3–4 feet in height and width. One of the Canadian Explorer series.

'**Dortmund**', kordesii, 9.4, medium red, Kordes, 1955.

Large, single red blooms with a showy white eye, borne in large clusters; light fragrance. Repeat-blooming, with a long season. Sets orange-red hips if not deadheaded. Dark, very glossy, disease-resistant foliage. Quite prickly. Hardy to Zone 4 or 5. Vigorous climbing growth, reaching 10–20 feet or more with support. Admired for its brilliant blooms and hardiness, 'Dortmund' won ADR honors in 1954 and a Portland Gold Medal in 1971.

'Dortmund', kordesii.

'**John Cabot**', kordesii, 9.4, medium red, Svejda, 1978.

Medium-size, cupped, semidouble deep-pink blooms with golden stamens, borne in large clusters. Some petals are marked with a distinctive small white stripe. Fragrant. Heavy spring bloom with late-summer repeat. Yellow-green, very disease-resistant foliage. Hardy to Zone 3. Upright, vigorous, arching growth; can be grown as a 6–foot shrub or 10–foot climber. 'John Cabot' was the first cultivar Felicitas Svejda introduced—the premier offering in the Canadian Explorer series bred at the Central Experimental Farm at Ottawa. It won a Certificate of Excellence from Britain's Royal National Rose Society in 1985. Unlike some cold-hardy roses, it performs well in warm climates too.

'John Cabot', kordesii.

'**William Baffin**', kordesii, 8.9, deep pink, Svejda, 1983.

Large, semidouble deep-pink flowers, borne in large clusters. Inner petals have a white streak in the center. Light fragrance. Good repeat bloom.

Glossy, medium-green foliage is disease-resistant. Hardy to Zone 3. Vigorous climbing growth reaching 8–12 feet; can also be grown as a large, lax shrub and makes a good tall hedge. Another high-rated rose in the Canadian Explorer series.

Other Shrubs

'Abraham Darby', shrub, 7.3, orange-pink, Austin, 1985. (Code name 'AUScot'; also called 'Abraham' and 'Country Darby'.)

Large, double, cupped apricot-pink blooms, yellowish-pink in the center; strong fruity fragrance. Good as a cut flower. Reliable repeat. Foliage is medium-green and leathery; has good resistance to powdery mildew but may need protection against blackspot and rust. Has extremely large prickles. Hardy to Zone 5 or 6. Vigorous and upright, reaching 5–7 feet or more. Slender, arching canes appreciate some support, and 'Abraham Darby' can be trained as a small climber or pillar rose (one parent is the climbing hybrid tea 'Aloha'). It's also a good candidate for pegging.

'Abraham Darby', shrub.

'A. MacKenzie', shrub, not rated, red blend, Svejda, 1985. (Also called 'Alexander MacKenzie'.)

Medium-size, double, cupped medium-red blooms with a lighter reverse, borne in clusters. Light raspberry fragrance; good repeat bloom. Glossy, leathery foliage is medium green and extremely resistant to blackspot, with good powdery mildew resistance. Purple prickles. Hardy to Zone 3. A tall, upright shrub, reaching a height of 4–6 feet, it can also be trained as a pillar rose or small climber. Makes a fine hedge. 'A. MacKenzie', one of the Canadian Explorer series, combines beauty, hardiness, and reliable repeat with admirable disease-resistance. Its ancestry includes 'New Dawn', 'Queen Elizabeth' (a parent), and the hybrid spinosissima 'Suzanne'.

'Basye's Purple Rose', shrub, not rated, mauve, Basye, 1968.

Small, velvety, single, intensely colored purple blooms with showy stamens; very good repeat; spicy clove fragrance. Rough, somewhat sparse medium-green foliage is extremely disease-resistant, with orange fall color. Many purple prickles. Hardy to Zone 4. Forms a dense, erect bush reaching 6–7 feet. Tolerates some shade. Retired Texas A&M professor Robert Basye's breeding goals included high disease-resistance

'Basye's Purple Rose', shrub.

and thornlessness as well as floral beauty. A cross between the species *Rosa rugosa* and *R. foliolosa*, 'Basye's Purple Rose' is a flop if judged by its prickliness but an outstanding achievement in resistance to blackspot and powdery mildew. Although it and other Basye shrubs 'Belinda's Dream' and 'Basye's Blueberry' aren't widely available, they can be ordered from specialty rose catalogs and are well worth searching for. Basye's hybridizing program continues at Texas A&M's Department of Horticultural Sciences, where the Robert E. Basye Endowed Chair in Rose Genetics has been created to help further the breeding of disease-resistant cultivars.

'Bonica', shrub, 8.5, medium pink, Meilland, 1985. (Code name 'MEIdomonac'; also called 'Bonica 82', 'Bonica Meidiland', and 'Démon'.)

Small, cupped, double rosettes with medium-pink center and lighter edges, borne in clusters; light green-apple fragrance; forms hips if not deadheaded. Good repeat; constantly in bloom, given a sunny location. Foliage is small, dark, semiglossy, and disease-resistant. Hardy to Zone 4 or 5. Vigorous, upright, somewhat spreading habit, reaching 3–5 feet in height.

'Bonica', shrub.

Tolerates some shade. In 1987 this easy-care rose was the first of its class to win AARS honors; it had already been a winner in the 1983 ADR trials. Its flowers are larger and hold their color better in cooler climates; blooms fade to white in hotter zones. In warm, wet climates 'Bonica' may require some protection from blackspot. A larger-flowered sport, 'Royal Bonica', was registered in 1994.

'Carefree Beauty', shrub, 8.5, medium pink, Buck, 1977.
(Code name 'BUCbi'; also called 'Audace'.)

'Carefree Beauty', shrub.

Large, semidouble light-rose flowers with slight fragrance. Good repeat; generous in bloom. Small olive-green foliage has excellent disease-resistance. Hardy to Zone 4 or 5. A vigorous, upright, spreading shrub that reaches a height of 5–6 feet. Makes a good hedge. 'Carefree Beauty'—the best-known of Dr. Griffith Buck's "prairie roses" and a cultivar he believed needed "no more care than a peony"—scored high in AARS trials but was downgraded because blooms were considered too floppy in some Southern climates. One of this rose's parents is 'Prairie Princess'.

'Carefree Delight', shrub, not rated, pink blend, Meilland, 1991.
(Code name 'MEIpotal'; also called 'Bingo Meidiland' and 'Bingo Meillandecor'.)

Small, single carmine-pink blooms with white eye and golden stamens, borne in large clusters. Reliable repeat and prolific bloom. Foliage is small, dark green, glossy, and very disease-resistant. Quite prickly. Hardy to Zone 4 or 5. A vigorous, arching shrub, growing 4–5 feet tall and about as wide. 'Carefree Delight' has covered itself in glory, winning awards from the AARS (1996) and ADR (1994) trials and gold medals at Paris and the Hague in 1992 and 1993, respectively.

'Carefree Wonder', shrub, 8.0, pink blend, Meilland, 1990.
(Code name 'MEIpitac'; also called 'Carefully Wonder' and 'Dynastie'.)

Large, double, cupped medium-pink flowers with a light-pink reverse, aging to medium pink, borne in sprays. Slight fragrance. Reliable repeat. Produces reddish-brown hips if not deadheaded. Medium-green semiglossy foliage has very good resistance to powdery mildew and moderate resistance to blackspot. Somewhat prickly. Hardy to Zone 4 or 5. Has a bushy, upright habit, reaching a height of 4–5 feet. Makes a good hedge. 'Carefree Wonder' was an AARS winner in 1991, the second shrub ever to receive the award.

'Flower Carpet', shrub, not rated, deep pink, Noack, 1991.
(Code name 'NOAtraum'; also called 'Blooming Carpet', 'Emera', 'Emera Pavement', 'Floral Carpet', 'Pink Flower Carpet', and 'Heidetraum'.)

Small, semidouble, cupped deep-pink flowers with a lighter reverse, borne in sprays of 15–25; slight fragrance. Reliable repeat and a profuse bloomer. Small, glossy, dark-green leaflets are very disease-resistant. Quite prickly. Hardy to Zone 5. A vigorous, low, dense, mounded shrub, reaching a height of 2–3 feet and a greater width. Tolerates some shade. Suitable as a groundcover rose, the heavily promoted 'Flower Carpet' has won five gold medals in Europe and honors in Germany's ADR trials (1990).

'Graham Thomas', shrub, 8.4, deep yellow, Austin, 1983.
(Code name 'AUSmas'; also called 'English Yellow' and 'Graham Stuart Thomas'.)

'Graham Thomas', shrub.

Medium-size, double, cupped yolk-yellow blooms; strong tea-rose fragrance; good for cutting. Repeat-blooming. Small medium-green, glossy foliage; moderately disease-resistant. Hardy to Zone 6. A vigorous, upright shrub, reaching a height of 5–7 feet in cooler climates but as much as 8–10 feet in warm regions. If it grows out of bounds in your garden, consider pegging it. 'Graham Thomas'—named for the world-renowned British rosarian—is one of David Austin's hybridizer favorites, combining true old-rose shape with modern coloration.

'**Hawkeye Belle**', shrub, 7.6, white, Buck, 1975.

Large, high-centered, double white blooms are tinted blush pink; good fragrance. Reliable repeat. Large dark-green, leathery foliage is very disease-resistant. Hardy to Zone 4 or 5. Forms a vigorous, upright shrub of 3–4 feet in height. 'Hawkeye Belle' inherits disease-resistance from both parents: one is the Buck shrub 'Prairie Princess', the other a hybrid of another Buck cultivar and the grandiflora 'Queen Elizabeth'.

'Hawkeye Belle', shrub.

'**Lavender Dream**', shrub, 8.3, mauve, Ilsink, 1984. (Code name 'INTerlav'.)

Medium-size, semidouble blooms of deep lilac-pink, borne in clusters. Reliable repeat; generous, continuous bloom. Light-green matte foliage is disease-resistant. Few prickles. Hardy to Zone 5. Bushy and well-branched, reaching 4–5 feet in height. An excellent landscape variety, though somewhat slow-growing, 'Lavender Dream' won the German ADR trials in 1987. It appreciates some shade in very hot climates.

'**Mary Rose**', shrub, 8.6, medium pink, Austin, 1983. (Code name 'AUSmary'; also called 'Country Marilou' and 'Marie Rose'.)

Large, cupped, very double warm-pink blooms; light fragrance; good for cutting. Very free-flowering, with reliable repeat. Medium-green matte foliage has good resistance to powdery mildew. Quite prickly. Hardy to Zone 4 or 5. Forms an upright, branching, bushy shrub 4–6 feet tall. 'Mary Rose' and 'Graham Thomas' were the first English roses to receive widespread public attention. Both were introduced at the Chelsea Flower Show in 1983. 'Mary Rose' produced the sports 'Winchester Cathedral' (white) and 'Redouté' (light pink).

'Pink Meidiland', shrub, 8.6, pink blend, Meilland, 1984.
(Code name 'MEIpoque'; also called 'Schloss Heidegg'.)

'Pink Meidiland', shrub.

Medium-size, single warm-pink flowers with showy white eye and stamens, borne in clusters. Reliable repeat, but bloom is somewhat sparse between spring and late-summer flushes. Forms red hips in fall if not deadheaded. Foliage is small, medium green, semiglossy, and disease-resistant. Quite prickly. Hardy to Zone 5. A vigorous and upright bush, reaching a height of 4–5 feet. Tolerates some shade. 'Pink Meidiland' won ADR honors in 1987 and is highly praised for its hardiness, disease-resistance, and excellence in the landscape. Others in the Meidiland series—including 'Red Meidiland', 'Scarlet Meidiland', 'Pearl Meidiland', and 'White Meidiland'—also make very good low-maintenance landscape shrubs.

'Prairie Princess', shrub, 8.4, orange-pink, Buck, 1972.

Large, semidouble coral-pink blooms with light fragrance. Reliable repeat; generous in flowering. Large, dark-green, leathery, disease-resistant foliage. Hardy to Zone 4 or 5. Vigorous upright growth, reaching about 5 feet in height. 'Prairie Princess' is one of Griffith Buck's better-known cultivars and a parent of his most widely sold rose, 'Carefree Beauty'. It also figures in the breeding of Meilland's 'Carefree Wonder'.

'Robusta', shrub, 9.6, medium red, Kordes, 1979.
(Code name 'KORgosa'.)

Medium-size, single scarlet blooms with golden stamens; constantly in flower. Light fruity fragrance. Dark, leathery disease-resistant foliage contrasts well with blooms. Forms an upright, bushy shrub 6–8 feet in height.

Tolerates some shade. Many prickles. Hardy to Zone 4 or 5. 'Robusta' won an ADR award in 1980 and makes an excellent easy-care hedge. Its rugose foliage resents spraying, and only light pruning is needed.

'**Sally Holmes**', shrub, 8.9, white, Holmes, 1976.

Large, creamy white, single flowers blushed with pink, with golden stamens, borne in large clusters; light fragrance. Reliable and rapid repeat; constantly in bloom. Foliage is glossy, dark green, and disease-resistant. Hardy to Zone 4. Vigorous, bushy, somewhat lax growth, reaching 7–10 feet in height and as much in spread. Can be trained as a pillar or climbing rose. One of the best-loved modern shrubs, 'Sally Holmes' was ARS members' top-rated large garden and exhibition rose for three years running, from 1994–1996. It also won gold medals in Baden-Baden, Germany, and Portland, Oregon, in 1980 and 1993, respectively. In the Deep South and other hot climates 'Sally Holmes' appreciates some afternoon shade. One of its parents is the hybrid musk 'Ballerina'.

'Sally Holmes', shrub.

Climbers and Ramblers

No rose truly climbs in the sense that vines do, with tendrils and other means of grasping onto supports. Instead, climbing and rambling roses produce long canes that gardeners can attach to fences, arches, and pillars. Even a single climber may have major garden impact, adding color and beauty high above the ground. The more horizontally its canes can be trained, the more blooms a climber will produce.

Ramblers bloom just once per year but in great profusion, bearing large clusters of small flowers. Their canes are flexible, quite long, and easy to train

'Belle Poitevine', hybrid rugosa, 8.5, medium pink

'Charles Albanel', hybrid rugosa, not rated, medium red

'Dart's Dash', hybrid rugosa, not rated, dark red

'David Thompson', hybrid rugosa, 8.5, medium red

'Delicata', hybrid rugosa, 8.3, light pink

'F. J. Grootendorst', hybrid rugosa, 7.7, medium red

'Frau Dagmar Hartopp' (also called 'Fru Dagmar Hastrupp'), hybrid rugosa, 8.5, medium pink

'Grootendorst Supreme', hybrid rugosa, 8.0, dark red

'Linda Campbell', hybrid rugosa, 7.4, medium red

'Martin Frobisher', hybrid rugosa, 7.2, light pink

'Mary Manners', hybrid rugosa, not rated, white

'Max Graf', hybrid rugosa, 7.2, pink blend

'Pink Grootendorst', hybrid rugosa, 7.8, medium pink

'Scabrosa', hybrid rugosa, 7.5, mauve

'Schneezwerg', hybrid rugosa, 7.6, white

'Thérèse Bugnet', hybrid rugosa, 8.1, medium pink

'Belinda', hybrid musk, 8.7, medium pink

'Bishop Darlington', hybrid musk, 7.5, apricot blend

'Clytemnestra', hybrid musk, 7.5, orange-pink

'Danaë', hybrid musk, 7.4, light yellow

'Erfurt', hybrid musk, 8.5, pink blend

'Felicia', hybrid musk, 8.3, pink blend

'Kathleen', hybrid musk, 8.8, light pink

'Lavender Lassie', hybrid musk, 8.0, mauve

'Nur Mahal', hybrid musk, not rated, medium red

'Penelope', hybrid musk, 8.8, light pink

'Prosperity', hybrid musk, 8.5, white

'Robin Hood', hybrid musk, 8.6, medium red

'Skyrocket', hybrid musk, 7.6, dark red

'Will Scarlet', hybrid musk, 8.1, medium red

'Heidelberg', kordesii, 8.7, medium red

'John Davis', kordesii, 8.5, medium pink

'Leverkusen', kordesii, 6.2, light yellow

'Louis Jolliet', kordesii, not rated, medium pink

'Parkdirektor Riggers', kordesii, not rated, dark red

'Alchymist', shrub, 8.0, apricot blend

'Amiga Mia', shrub, 7.3, medium pink

'Applejack', shrub, 7.9, pink blend

'Basye's Blueberry', shrub, not rated, medium pink

'Belinda's Dream', shrub, not rated, medium pink

'Belle Story', shrub, 8.9, light pink

'Bredon', shrub, 7.9, apricot blend

'Captain Samuel Holland', shrub, not rated, medium red

'Cardinal Hume', shrub, 7.7, mauve

'Cerise Bouquet', shrub, 8.1, deep pink

'Charles Rennie Mackintosh', shrub, not rated, pink blend

'Charmian', shrub, 8.9, medium pink

'Cherry Meidiland', shrub, not rated, red blend

'Constance Spry', shrub, 8.5, light pink

'Country Dancer', shrub, 8.4, deep pink

'Cuthbert Grant', shrub, not rated, dark red

'Distant Drums', shrub, 8.1, mauve

'Dorcas', shrub, not rated, pink blend

'Eddie's Crimson', shrub, 9.1, medium red

'Eddie's Jewel', shrub, not rated, medium red

'First Light', shrub, not rated, light pink, AARS

'Geranium', shrub, 8.3, medium red

'Golden Celebration', shrub, not rated, deep yellow

'Golden Wings', shrub, 8.9, light yellow

'Heritage', shrub, 8.3, light pink

'Honeysweet', shrub, not rated, orange-pink

'John Franklin', shrub, not rated, medium red

'Jude the Obscure', shrub, not rated, medium yellow

'Leander', shrub, 8.3, apricot blend

'Lillian Austin', shrub, 8.6, orange-pink

'Lillian Gibson', shrub, not rated, medium pink

'Lucetta', shrub, 7.3, apricot blend

'Maigold', shrub, 7.6, deep yellow

'Nevada', shrub, 8.8, white

'Oranges & Lemons', shrub, not rated, orange blend

'Perdita', shrub, 7.8, apricot blend

'Prairie Harvest', shrub, not rated, light yellow

'Queen Margrethe', shrub, not rated, light pink

'Red Simplicity', shrub, 7.3, medium red

'Redouté', shrub, not rated, light pink

'St. Swithun', shrub, not rated, light pink

'Scarlet Meidiland', shrub, 7.6, medium red

'Sea Foam', shrub, 7.8, white

'Shropshire Lass', shrub, not rated, light pink

'Sir Clough', shrub, not rated, deep pink

'Smarty', shrub, not rated, light pink

'Sparrieshoop', shrub, 7.9, light pink

'Symphony', shrub, not rated, light yellow

'Tamora', shrub, not rated, apricot blend

'The Alexandra Rose', shrub, not rated, pink blend

'The Countryman', shrub, 7.8, medium pink

'The Herbalist', shrub, not rated, deep pink

'Tradescant', shrub, not rated, dark red

'Wenlock', shrub, 7.2, medium red

'Windrush', shrub, 7.8, light yellow

'Yellow Button', shrub, not rated, yellow blend

for growth on fences, arbors, and other supports. Climbers are usually repeat-blooming and come in many classes because, in addition to those plants hybridized and introduced as climbers, many kinds of roses produce climbing sports. Thus you can choose climbing miniatures, hybrid teas, polyanthas, floribundas, and grandifloras, and among the old roses, climbing Bourbons, Chinas, hybrid perpetuals, mosses, and teas. Then there are the Noisettes, most of which have extremely long canes that are perfect for training as climbers. The class of large-flowered climbers encompasses the many cultivars that are not sports from roses in other classes.

Although gardeners in the coldest climates have fewer choices when it comes to climbers because of the difficulty of protecting long canes from winter-kill, a number of roses in the very hardy class kordesii are usually grown as climbers. Several such hardy varieties are profiled in the preceding shrub section.

Climbers

'**City of York**', large-flowered climber, 8.6, white, Tantau, 1945.
(Also called 'Direktor Benschop'.)

Large, cupped, semidouble, creamy-white, slightly ruffled flowers with golden-yellow stamens, produced in large clusters of 7–15; in many climates, once-blooming but generously and over a long season; may repeat in warmer regions. Strong fragrance. Well-covered in glossy, medium-green, leathery foliage. Quite disease-resistant and hardy. Sets hips if not deadheaded. Hardy to Zone 5. Vigorous, flexible, moderately prickly canes reach a height of 15–20 feet. Arguably the best white large-flowered climber, 'City of York' is the only rose in its class to have won the American Rose Society's rarely bestowed National Gold Medal Certificate for Outstanding Performance (1950).

'City of York', large-flowered climber.

'**Compassion**', large-flowered climber, 8.7, orange-pink, Harkness, 1972.
(Also called 'Belle de Londres'.)

Large, double salmon-pink blooms with apricot-orange shadings and good hybrid-tea form. Generous in flower production, with sweet fragrance. Makes a good cut flower. Foliage is large, dark green, and glossy; disease-resistant; large prickles. Hardy to Zone 4 or 5. Bushy, rather stiff growth to 8–10 feet in height; can also be grown as a large shrub. 'Compassion' won three gold medals in Europe, honors in the stringent German ADR trials in 1976, and England's Edland Fragrance Medal in 1973.

'**New Dawn**', large-flowered climber, 8.5, light pink, Dreer, 1930.
(Also called 'Everblooming Dr. W. Van Fleet' and 'The New Dawn'.)

'New Dawn', large-flowered climber.

Medium-size, cupped, double soft-pink flowers fade to white; light apple fragrance. Reliable repeat. Dark-green glossy leaflets with very good disease-resistance; large prickles. Hardy to Zone 4 or 5. Vigorous, growing 12–20 feet in height. Named World's Favorite Rose in 1997. Renowned for its delicate beauty, ease of care, and healthy foliage—and also for being the first plant ever patented. 'New Dawn' is a repeat-blooming, slightly less vigorous sport of 'Dr. W. Van Fleet', which was hybridized by its name-sake (who wanted to call the rose 'Daybreak'). The patent was granted to Dreer, who introduced the sport discovered by a New Jersey landscape gar-dener. 'New Dawn' can tolerate some shade and perform well on four to five hours of sun. In hot climates flowering will slow or stop at the height of summer. A sport, 'Awakening', discovered in Czechoslovakia in the 1930s and reintroduced by Peter Beales of England in 1992, has twice as many petals and quartered blooms.

'**Parade**', large-flowered climber, 8.1, deep pink, Boerner, 1953.

Large, cupped, deep-rose-pink double flowers of old-rose shape; damask fragrance; repeat-blooming and free-flowering; produces orange hips if not deadheaded. A good cut flower. Well-clad in glossy, disease-resistant foliage. Hardy to Zone 6 or 7. A vigorous, shrubby climber attaining about 8 feet in height and 12 feet in width; can be grown as a large, lax shrub. One parent was a 'New Dawn' seedling, which likely contributed to this climber's disease-resistance.

'Parade', large-flowered climber.

'**Sombreuil**', climbing tea, 8.8, white, Robert, 1850.

Large, very double, flat, quartered creamy-white blooms often tinged pink; very fragrant, with hints of lemon, tea, and apple. Reliable repeat. Good for cutting. Foliage is leathery, medium green, and disease-resistant. Moderately prickly. Hardy to Zone 6. Vigorous, climbing growth, reaching a height of 12–15 feet. 'Sombreuil' has been the subject of a great deal of speculation, as many rosarians believe that the variety now offered for sale by that name is not the original. Others suggest that plants sold in Europe and North America are two different cultivars. Whatever the case, the 'Sombreuil' available here and now is a lush, sweetly scented rose well worth growing. Stephen Scanniello, rosarian for the Brooklyn Botanic Garden, called it "one of the best climbing tea roses and one of the most beautiful roses ever created."

Climbing Miniatures

'**Jeanne Lajoie**', climbing miniature, 9.3, medium pink, Sima, 1975.

Small, double, high-centered medium-pink blooms with a darker reverse. Reliable repeat; constantly in bloom. Slight fragrance. Small, dark-green glossy foliage with good disease-resistance. Hardy to Zone 5 or 6. Upright, well-branched, climbing growth to 6–8 feet; long, slender canes are proportionate to shapely flowers. Given the ARS Award of Excellence in 1977, 'Jeanne Lajoie' is highly praised for its beauty and exceptional floral profusion. A good choice for pegging.

'Jeanne Lajoie', climbing miniature.

'Nozomi', climbing miniature, 8.0, light pink, Onodera, 1968.
(Also called 'Heideröslein Nozomi'.)

Small, single, flat, pearly pink blooms appear in great trusses; slight fragrance. Disease-resistant foliage is small, dark green, and glossy; tinged with purple when new. Once-blooming but with an extended season of flowering. Hardy to Zone 5. Despite its classification as a climber, the dense and spreading 'Nozomi' is often used as a trailing groundcover rose. Without support, it grows 2–3 feet tall and up to 6 feet wide; plants trained on supports can reach 5–6 feet. Perhaps because of its China ancestry, this rose performs well in warm climates.

Ramblers

'Albéric Barbier', rambler, 7.5, light yellow, Barbier, 1900.

Yellow buds open to large, creamy-white double flowers with yellow centers, borne in clusters over a long season; green-apple fragrance. Once-blooming. Glossy dark foliage with very good disease-resistance; fairly prickly. Hardy to Zone 5 or 6. Vigorous, flexible growth, reaching 15–20 feet or more. Tolerates some shade. One of the best ramblers, although it should

'Albéric Barbier', rambler.

probably be classed with the hybrid wichuraianas because of its *R. wichuraiana* parent. Its other parent, the tea 'Shirley Hibberd', may have contributed its ability to tolerate hot climates.

'**Chevy Chase**', rambler, 7.5, deep red, Hansen, 1939.

'*Chevy Chase*', rambler.

Small, cherry-red, very double blooms in clusters of 10–20. Fragrant; once-blooming. Soft, light-green, crinkled foliage; many prickles. Less hardy than most of its class, but unlike other red ramblers, very disease-resistant. Hardy to Zone 6 or 7. A vigorous climber, to 15 feet. 'Chevy Chase' received the ARS Dr. W. Van Fleet Medal in 1941. One parent is the species *Rosa soulieana* from southwestern China; the other is a polyantha descended from the tender China rose 'Cramoisi Supérieur'.

'Alexandre Girault', large-flowered climber, not rated, pink blend

'Altissimo', large-flowered climber, 9.5, medium red

'Blaze', large-flowered climber, 7.2, medium red

'Clair Matin', large-flowered climber, 9.0, medium pink

'Mme. Grégoire Staechelin', large-flowered climber, 7.7, pink blend

'Red Fountain', large-flowered climber, 7.8, dark red

'Rhonda', large-flowered climber, 8.4, medium pink

'Royal Sunset', large-flowered climber, 9.2, apricot blend

'Temptation', large-flowered climber, not rated, medium red

'Fred Loads', climbing floribunda, 8.5, orange-red

'Gloire de Dijon', climbing tea, 7.2, orange-pink

'Lady Hillingdon, Climbing', climbing tea, not rated, yellow blend

'Mrs. Herbert Stevens, Climbing', climbing hybrid tea, not rated, white

'Old Blush, Climbing', climbing China, 8.1, medium pink

'Tausendschön', hybrid multiflora, 8.5, pink blend

'Cécile Brünner, Climbing', climbing polyantha, 8.3, light pink

'Pink Cameo', climbing miniature, 7.6, medium pink

'Pinkie, Climbing', climbing polyantha, 7.4, medium pink

'Red Cascade', climbing miniature, 7.0, dark red, ARS Award of Excellence

'American Pillar', rambler, 7.6, pink blend

'Lady Gay', rambler, not rated, orange-pink

ongoing

rose care

The Essentials

- How and When to Water
- Understanding Fertilizers
- Pruning
- Rose Hardiness and Winter Protection

If you've planted your roses in good soil and plenty of sunshine, they already have much of what they need to flourish. Now it's up to you to provide water and fertilizer, to prune your roses periodically, to give them winter protection if you garden in a cold climate or are growing tender varieties, and to prevent diseases and insects from getting the upper hand.

That may sound like a lot of work, but it doesn't have to be. Whenever possible, this section will offer labor-saving tips and suggestions to help you spend more time enjoying your roses and less time tending them.

It's important to understand that a healthy rose—one that is well-sited, well-watered, and getting the nutrients it needs in the right amounts—is better able to resist disease and endure insect invasion. It's also much more productive and beautiful. This part of the book will show you how to build the toughest, healthiest rosebushes possible. The next part will present detailed information on coping with diseases and insect pests.

How and When to Water

Sturdy though they are, roses are largely made up of water, and like us, they can't thrive if they aren't properly hydrated. Water helps drive plant growth and the development of flowers, and a lack of water—especially during times of rapid growth—weakens a plant and makes it more susceptible to disease and insect damage.

Certain tough roses can survive without fertilizer or pruning: native species roses prove the point, as do cultivated varieties that may be found growing untended in old cemeteries and on abandoned homesteads. But no rose can live without adequate water.

Generally speaking, roses need about an inch or two of water per week during the growing season in order to reach their potential. The hotter it is, the sandier the soil, and the more sun they get, the more water they'll need. If nature doesn't provide that through slow and steady rainfall (during brief spells of heavy rain the soil isn't able to take up much water), you'll have to.

The best method is one that allows you to water plants—whether roses, perennials, or your lawn—deeply and infrequently (once or twice a week, as weather dictates) rather than shallowly and often. Deep and infrequent watering encourages roots to grow deeply in search of water; shallow, frequent watering keeps feeder roots concentrated in the first few inches of the soil, where they readily dry out.

If you have only a handful of roses or a small garden, you may want to water by hand with a hose. It can take a surprisingly long time, though, because the soil must be moistened as deep as the roses' root zone—which can extend 18 inches or more below the surface. Apply a gentle stream, and avoid splashing soil—which may harbor fungi—onto foliage.

But if you don't have time to stand around while mosquitoes attack your legs and arms, install a soaker hose, with thousands of tiny pores from which water slowly seeps. A more expensive and elegant solution is to install drip irrigation: a series of small taps or bubblers that deliver water to each plant or section of the garden bed. Do-it-yourself systems are more economical than those installed by landscapers, but if your garden is very large, you may want a professional to set things up.

One advantage of both soaker hoses and drip irrigation is that they deliver water directly to the soil, where it can be quickly taken up by plants' roots, without splashing and with little or no waste. Sprinklers that spray water through the air waste a great deal because of evaporation and the inaccuracy of their delivery.

In addition, if you live in a wet climate where blackspot or rust is a serious fungal problem, you don't want to wet the roses' foliage any more than necessary because the spores germinate on wet leaves. In contrast, the spores of the fungus that causes powdery mildew won't germinate when wet. So if you live in a dry climate where roses are plagued more by powdery mildew than blackspot, spraying your roses with water periodically can actually help prevent disease.

The best time of day to water is early morning, when the temperature is lower and less water is lost to evaporation. Watering in the evening isn't a good idea; leaves that stay wet all night provide a perfect environment for the development of blackspot, and even if the leaves haven't been wetted, high nighttime humidity in the plants' immediate environment encourages powdery mildew.

Part 2 pointed out the importance of mulch. A 1- to 2-inch layer of composted bark, chopped leaves, composted straw, mushroom compost, ground corncobs, or other organic matter helps keep soil moist and cool and—by preventing the top layer of soil from crusting—permits water to penetrate more readily. As it decays, mulch adds a steady trickle of organic matter to the soil, and it cuts down greatly on weed germination because it prevents sunlight from reaching the soil surface. Those weeds that do sprout are much easier to pull from loose, soft, mulched soil than from bare ground. As you make your garden rounds, keep an eye out for bare patches of soil so you can add mulch as needed.

Understanding Fertilizers

Most roses benefit from regular applications of fertilizer—but what kind? The shelves are filled with a huge array of products: special rose formulas, general-purpose fertilizers, water-soluble crystals, time-release granules, all-organic products, and so on. Choosing among them can be confusing.

But since roses can't read, they won't know the difference between the 15-15-15 granules you bought in a fifty-pound sack at the agricultural co-op and the special rose fertilizer that costs ten times as much per pound and has pretty pictures on the package. The important thing is that you apply what your roses need—no more and no less.

All balanced fertilizers use a series of three numbers to indicate what percentage of nitrogen (N), phosphorus (P), and potassium (K) they include, and the chemicals are always listed in that order: N, P, K. Thus, a product labeled 10-10-10 has 10 percent nitrogen, 10 percent phosphorus, and 10 percent potassium. The rest of the product consists mainly of fillers.

Some fertilizers contain only one of those three elements. Take, for example, ammonium nitrate, which is labeled 33-0-0. It contains about 33.5 percent nitrogen and no phosphorus or potassium. Superphosphate is labeled 0-20-0 and contains 20 percent phosphorus but no nitrogen or potassium.

Many balanced fertilizers—especially the more expensive formulations—also contain trace minerals: chemicals such as boron, molybdenum, and zinc that roses need only in small amounts. It's good insurance to apply a fertilizer with trace elements at least occasionally.

Part 2 explained the necessity of having your soil tested in order to get specific fertilizer recommendations appropriate to your garden. Let's say, for example, that the soil in your rose bed is already quite high in phosphorus and potassium. In such a case, the soil-test recommendation might be to apply a specific amount of nitrogen in the form of ammonium nitrate to each rosebush at particular intervals during the growing season.

Don't assume that if a moderate amount of fertilizer is good, more is better. Applying more than your roses need can weaken them just as a shortage can. Too much nitrogen, for example, encourages soft, sappy plant growth that rings a dinner bell for insects and foliar diseases. An excess of potassium can cause leaf yellowing and wilting of young shoots. So use chemical fertilizers only in the amounts the soil test recommends.

Too much fertilizer can also cause a toxic buildup of salts in the soil, which can be especially damaging when the ground is dry (or if drainage is poor). For this reason inorganic fertilizer should never be applied to dry soil. When it is applied, it should be watered in deeply so that the solution of chemical salts that meets the roots is dilute and will not damage the plant.

Once you have your soil-test results in hand and know what nutrients you need to add and in what proportions, you still have to select what form to use. Water-soluble formulas reach plants almost immediately (all nutrients, no matter what their origins, are delivered to the plant dissolved in water) but must be applied relatively frequently. Time-release fertilizers can save you trouble but are often relatively expensive. If you use a time-release product, keep in mind that it will break down more quickly in warm, wet weather. Apply it early enough in the season that it won't continue stimulating growth in fall, when roses need to start shutting down for the winter.

Organics

Some gardeners prefer to do without commercial chemical products entirely, instead using natural materials such as fish emulsion or meal, blood meal, bone meal, alfalfa meal, cottonseed meal, compost, and manure to feed their roses. Certainly gardeners in past centuries were able to grow exemplary plants without the use of laboratory-produced fertilizers.

One of the best arguments for using organics—whether in addition to or instead of chemical fertilizers—is that an increase in organic matter improves soil health. That is, organic products nourish the soil while they nourish the rose.

Organic matter, as part 2 explained, improves soil tilth, making the soil easier for you to tend and for roots to grow in. Organics also enhance the soil's ability to retain nutrients and make them available to plants. Thus, fertilizers added to a soil high in organic content are more effective. In short, every healthy rose garden needs a steady supply of organic matter.

Nutrients in organic matter are released slowly because soil organisms must break them down first in order for them to become available to the plant. This time lag shouldn't pose problems for healthy roses, but if a plant is suffering a specific deficiency—or enjoying a period of rapid growth—organics alone may not be able to supply the needed nutrients quickly enough. One faster-acting way to deliver organic fertilizers is to make a "tea," or solution, of manure, fish meal, alfalfa meal, or another amendment in water. To make a tea, suspend a burlap bag filled with the fertilizer of choice in a large plastic trash can filled with water. Cover with a tight-fitting lid (teas are usually fairly strong-smelling), and let the mixture steep for several days. Then water plants with the resulting solution. The odor will dissipate fairly quickly once the tea sinks into the ground.

Naturally produced fertilizers are also typically less strong than commercial ones, so you'll have to apply more blood meal (13 percent nitrogen) or fish meal (10 percent nitrogen), for example, than ammonium nitrate (33.5 percent nitrogen) to get the same results. Follow package directions closely: used in excess, even natural fertilizers can burn plant roots.

Whatever you use, start fertilizing in early spring, after the danger of frost has passed, and stop about six weeks before the first frost date, giving plants a chance to slow down as the dormant season approaches.

Many rosarians also swear by Epsom salts, or magnesium sulfate, believing it helps encourage roses to produce new basal breaks. A typical recommendation would be $\frac{1}{4}$ cup Epsom salts per large, established bush, scratched lightly into the mulch or soil surface and watered in well. Some experts apply Epsom salts just after pruning; others wait till the end of the first spring bloom cycle.

Pruning

New rose gardeners tend to feel nervous about pruning, worrying that they'll damage their bushes by trimming them and feeling unsure about just what to cut and where. You needn't worry: roses are forgiving plants. At worst, you'll make them look bad or reduce the year's flowering.

Pruning is really a matter of common sense, once you realize why we prune: to remove dead, diseased, and weak wood; to increase air circulation and thus discourage disease; to shape the plant; and to stimulate new growth and flower production.

Pruning does all of these things, and it's one of the best ways to improve your roses' health and vitality. A few general guidelines apply to all classes of roses, old or modern; beyond that, various kinds of roses have additional requirements.

There are no hard and fast rules about when to prune. One traditional piece of advice is to wait until the forsythias bloom. Some rosarians—especially those in relatively warm climates, where a late cold snap tends to do more damage—don't take up the shears until the danger of frost has passed. Others find that certain classes of roses, including most modern roses, can be pruned several weeks before the last-frost date, when the leaf buds are just beginning to swell. The chief danger of early pruning is that mild late-winter weather may strongly stimulate new growth, which can be nipped by a hard freeze.

If you're new to roses, probably the best advice on timing can be had from your county agricultural extension agent or a local consulting rosarian (CR) affiliated with the American Rose Society (see the appendix for information on contacting the ARS to get in touch with CRs in your area).

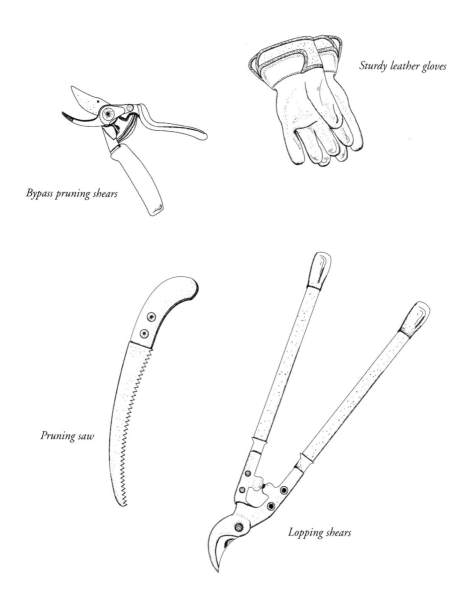

Sturdy leather gloves

Bypass pruning shears

Pruning saw

Lopping shears

Pruning shears   They're available in two styles: bypass and anvil. Bypass pruners have a curved blade and work with a scissor action. Rosarians prefer them because they make sharper, cleaner cuts. In the anvil type, a flat blade meets a broad, flat surface, and this sort of pruner can crush rose canes rather than cleanly slice them.

Expect to pay thirty to forty dollars or more for a good pair of bypass shears. Look for a brand that sells replacement parts and whose shears can be disassembled so blades can be sharpened and cleaned. Such a pair can last a lifetime, so it's well worth the initial expense. Keep your pruners free of rust by cleaning them as needed with WD-40 and a pot-scrubbing pad.

Lopping shears   A good pair of loppers—a scissorlike tool with relatively short blades and long handles—makes it much easier to cut the large, tough canes that vigorous roses develop after a few years in the ground. If your roses are newly planted, you can probably get by with just a pair of shears the first spring you prune. After that, you'll find the loppers come in quite handy.

Pruning saw   Sometimes it's impossible to get the blades on a pair of loppers or shears into a tight space where a cane should be removed. That's where your pruning saw comes in. An inexpensive tool with a narrow blade, it allows you to cut off large canes cleanly, without leaving a stub that can serve as an entry point for disease.

Sturdy leather gloves and arm protection   Even those who adore roses sometimes curse them at pruning time. Wear a pair of tough, puncture-proof gloves and a jacket with long sleeves, and you'll avoid the bloodshed these prickly beauties can cause. You'll also protect yourself from "rose fever," an infection caused when the fungus *Sporothrix schenckii*—which lives in soil and on decaying plant material—is transmitted via a thorn puncture or other injury.

Guidelines for Pruning All Roses

1. Use sharp, clean pruning shears. Disinfect your shears as you move from bush to bush by dipping the blades in a solution of one part household bleach to nine parts water, then wiping them dry. This helps prevent the spread of fungal and bacterial diseases.

2. Cut at a 45-degree angle, about $1/4$ inch above an outward-facing bud eye, the reddish swelling from which a new cane will grow. The cut should slant away from the bud. Pruning stimulates the bud to grow, and since you've cut to an outward-facing one, the cane will grow out rather than toward the center of the bush. (If a rose is growing too wide, however, and you'd like to narrow it, cut to inward-facing buds—but watch for and correct overcrowding that could reduce air circulation.) In some varieties and on older canes the bud eyes may be more difficult to spot. Look for slight "scars" on the cane that mark where leaves used to be attached. Bud eyes can be found immediately above those scars.

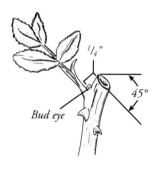

Correct placement and angle of pruning cuts.

3. Entirely remove all dead or dying canes. They'll be dry and brittle, shriveled, or dark brown or black. Cut them off where they emerge from the crown of the plant, leaving no stub. Also trim away any damaged or broken wood and diseased areas of canes: those with irregular swellings or growths, wounds or lesions, or dark, blotchy discoloration.

4. Always cut down to healthy pith, the tissue inside the cane. It will be creamy white or a light tan color. It's normal for the pith of older wood to be somewhat discolored. If cane-boring insects are a pest in your area (your county agricultural extension agent or the local rose society can tell you), seal the cut ends with a few drops of white glue or carpenter's glue.

5. If two canes rub against each other, remove one. Rubbing can damage canes and invite disease and insect pests, and canes that grow close together can reduce air circulation.

Prune down to healthy pith that's creamy white or light tan.

6. Remove all canes that are noticeably thin or twiggy (except when the entire bush is composed of spindly canes—for example, in a polyantha). Puny canes won't be able to support heavy blooms once flowering starts.

7. If roses are grafted, remove any suckers—shoots growing from the understock, not the named variety. If the graft is planted below ground, dig down gently with your gloved hands to make sure of the shoot's origin. Suckers should be clipped or torn off where they emerge from the rootstock. If they're left alone, they can quickly overwhelm the slower-growing cultivated variety.

8. Bag and throw away all the trimmings. Don't add them to your compost pile.

Pruning Modern Roses: Hybrid Teas, Grandifloras, Floribundas, Polyanthas, and Miniatures

When pruning modern roses with an upright bushy form rather than a spreading shrubby form, one of the primary goals is to open the center of the bush to improve air circulation and discourage disease. These roses bloom on both old wood (canes) and new and most should be pruned more severely than shrubby cultivars or climbers, both modern and old.

PRUNING A HYBRID TEA

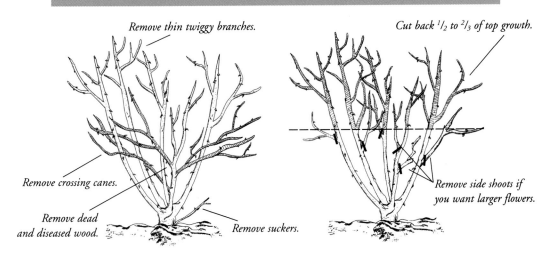

Remove thin twiggy branches.

Cut back $^1/_2$ to $^2/_3$ of top growth.

Remove crossing canes.

Remove dead and diseased wood.

Remove suckers.

Remove side shoots if you want larger flowers.

This usually means you'll cut away one-half to two-thirds of the bush's height and reduce the number of canes. The harder you prune, that is, the shorter you cut the bush and the more canes you remove, the larger and fewer the flowers will be. Rose exhibitors who want grand flowers may leave only three to four vigorous canes; those looking for a fuller show in the garden may leave five or six—perhaps more—and more side shoots. Only an extremely vigorous bush can support a large number of canes, so if you're in doubt, leave fewer canes.

In cold climates these roses will have more winter damage and thus need harder pruning—down to a height of 12 to 14 inches or so (even shorter if winter-kill has been more extensive). Warm-climate gardeners tend to leave canes 18 to 24 inches tall or more, up to perhaps four feet in southern California.

In frost-free climates pruning rosebushes and removing their leaves are methods of inducing dormancy, giving the plants a brief rest from growth and flower production that they wouldn't otherwise have. Gardeners in such climates often prune in January or February, priming their plants for heavy flowering 10 to 12 weeks later.

When pruning hybrid teas, many gardeners remove all the side shoots emerging from the main canes. Others leave the sturdiest of the side shoots, or lateral growth, producing a fuller bush. It's a matter of personal preference. Good-size side shoots may be left on grandifloras and floribundas, which flower in clusters rather than one bloom to a stem.

New shoots that will bear this year's flowers can be no bigger than the canes they're growing from, so experts often advise removing all growth that's thinner than a number two pencil. Thinner stems may not be able to support the coming season's blooms.

In all cases, remove old, woody canes that are more than three or four years old. That helps encourage the growth of basal breaks (new canes).

Standard hybrid teas, grandifloras, and floribundas—those grafted to a small treelike stem—should be pruned just as their more earthbound cousins are.

Miniatures should be thinned and cut back by one-third to one-half.

Small, twiggy polyanthas benefit from moderate pruning. After removing any undesirable growth or dead wood, shorten them to about two-thirds of their end-of-season height.

Pruning Repeat-flowering Shrub and Landscape Roses

Have you ever seen a forsythia—an arching, fountain-shaped shrub—trimmed flat across the top as though it were a boxwood? That's a perfect example of what not to do when pruning shrub roses.

Pay attention to their natural shape: some are stiff and upright, some arching, some dense and compact, and others lax and spreading. After you've removed sick, dead, or crossing canes and trimmed back any dead wood, as described above, your task is to enhance the beauty of the bush by pruning in accordance with its form.

If the plant has become a crowded thicket, selectively remove some of the older or weaker canes. That will both increase air circulation and encourage new and vigorous growth.

If the plant is quite old and overgrown, you may want to revitalize it by removing no more than one-third of the oldest canes each year. At the end of three years, you'll have a healthy plant with nothing but strong new growth.

In their first couple of seasons most shrubs should be left unpruned. Wait and see what sort of shape emerges—unless they're taking over the garden and need a controlling hand.

PRUNING A SHRUB

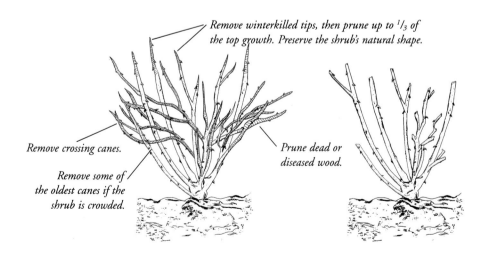

Remove winterkilled tips, then prune up to $^1/_3$ of the top growth. Preserve the shrub's natural shape.

Remove crossing canes.

Remove some of the oldest canes if the shrub is crowded.

Prune dead or diseased wood.

When pruning shrubs, it's not necessary to reduce the length of the canes as much as you would with hybrid teas. Once you've cut away anything winter-killed or diseased, you have a lot of leeway: some gardeners prune just the tips of the canes; others routinely remove as much as one-third of the growth. Experiment to see which approach gives you better results.

Species roses and their hybrids should be allowed to assume their natural shape and pruned as much or as little as you deem necessary to keep them in bounds. For those that bloom only once, major pruning should be left until flowering is over, unless you want the plant to form hips. In that case, you'll leave the spent blooms on the shrub and will need to prune lightly before the next spring's flowering.

Pruning Old Garden Roses

Most old roses are shrubby in form and can be pruned using the guidelines described above. There are a few additional considerations, though.

Old European roses that bloom just once a year (the albas, gallicas, damasks, centifolias, and mosses) flower on old wood, so except for removing dead or diseased canes, you should delay pruning until after they bloom. Once their season of bloom has passed, shape them as little or as much as you like. Some rosarians cut them back by as much as a third; others prefer to trim only the tips—or nothing at all. As with other shrubs, you should thin overgrown plants, and cut out some of the oldest canes if you want to spur new growth. These roses need not be pruned each year, except for removal of dead, damaged, and diseased wood.

Repeat-flowering old roses—for example, Bourbons, Portlands, and hybrid perpetuals—can be pruned before flowering and cut back a little harder since they, like modern repeaters, bloom on both new and old wood. Bourbons and hybrid perpetuals are often prone to disease, so it's desirable to keep their centers open.

The most tender repeating old roses—the Chinas, teas, and Noisettes—should be treated with the same restraint shown to shrub roses. Cut shrubby ones back by no more than one-third once you've thinned them. Treat those trained as climbers (for example, most Noisettes) as you would other repeat-flowering climbers. Don't prune these three classes until after the last spring frost; they start growing again immediately after pruning, and new growth may be damaged by freezing temperatures.

Pruning Climbers and Ramblers

Like shrubs, climbers and ramblers need a few seasons to become established. Don't prune them, except to remove dead or diseased wood, until their third year in your garden.

THE CONTROVERSIAL HEDGE-TRIMMING TECHNIQUE

Now that you've learned the basics of traditional pruning practices, you might want to know about the fascinating research the Royal National Rose Society conducted for several years at its test gardens in St. Albans, England. Comparable beds of hybrid teas, floribundas, and grandifloras were pruned in one of three different ways: (1) in the traditional fashion, (2) by rough pruning—that is, cutting canes to a given length without opening centers, cutting out weak wood, or paying attention to cutting above bud eyes, and (3) with hedge trimmers, perhaps the ultimate rough-pruning tools.

The surprising result was that roses roughly pruned or cut with hedge trimmers performed just as well as, and in some cases better than, those painstakingly pruned in the usual way.

Nonetheless, there are drawbacks to rough cutting. Vigorous plants will eventually develop crowded centers, which may invite disease. And if the oldest and weakest wood is never removed, bushes may produce few new canes. For these reasons, as well as the weight of tradition, not many rosarians have adopted this method. Most would rather spend a bit more time pruning and take the opportunity to determine their plants' ultimate shape. In fact, the Royal National Rose Society itself still teaches beginners the traditional way.

But if you'd like to try this approach in your garden, why not? Plan to spend a little time at least every two or three years thinning your roses' centers.

Although no shrub roses were used in these studies, it's likely that hedge trimmers could be used on them without ill effects. Do avoid giving plants a buzz-cut across the top: trim in a way that preserves shrubs' natural shape.

Ramblers bloom only once a year; most of the cultivars categorized as climbers bloom repeatedly.

In both cases pruning techniques are the same; it's the timing that differs. As with once-blooming shrubs, cut back ramblers after spring bloom. Prune repeating climbers in early spring, when you prune modern repeating roses and shrubs.

Trim the tips of the canes, and reduce side shoots, or laterals, from the main canes to about 3 to 6 inches. Most flowers will spring from these laterals, and you'll see a lot more bloom if they're trimmed back and stimulated to grow.

Day-to-day Pruning

Every time you cut blooms for the house or deadhead (trim off spent flowers), you're pruning, spurring the plant to further growth and bloom. If the bush is once-blooming, you may choose not to deadhead. Leaving spent flowers on the bush will in many cases lead to the formation of hips. They're attractive and edible to both birds and man (ripe hips are high in vitamin C and can be turned into tea or jelly and otherwise used in recipes if they haven't been sprayed with chemicals), and allowing them to mature gives the bush the signal that it's time to slow down and prepare for dormancy.

If the bush is repeat-flowering, cease deadheading six weeks before the first frost. You don't want to stimulate the plant to start producing tender growth when cold weather is near.

Rose Hardiness and Winter Protection

North America is divided into winter-hardiness zones determined by average annual minimum winter temperatures, from Zone 1, with temperatures below −50°F, to Zone 10, whose winter minimum is 30°F. If you're not sure what zone you're in, check the USDA Plant Hardiness Zone Map on page 160. Because the zones are based on average minimums, you may occasionally see colder temperatures.

Roses' winter hardiness varies widely: the old European albas and damasks are hardy to Zone 4 (some to Zone 3); rugosa hybrids and the modern shrubs developed by Agriculture Canada to Zones 3 and 4; many hybrid teas to

Zone 6 (with hardier and tenderer exceptions); most Noisettes and Chinas to Zone 7.

Obviously, then, your roses' need for winter care will depend on what they are and where you are. Gardeners in the colder zones employ a variety of plant-saving techniques, from simple to quite complex, that enable them to grow varieties that aren't hardy in their area.

If you'd like your rose garden to be as easy-care as possible, stick to varieties that can endure your zone's weather or that will need only minimal safeguarding. Fortunately, gardeners in frigid Zones 3 and 4 have more rosy choices than ever (see part 3 for recommended hardy cultivars).

A wide variety of roses can be grown in Zones 5 and 6. The old European roses and many shrubs and species are completely hardy in those areas; in Zone 5 some floribundas and most hybrid teas, grandifloras, and hybrid musks need sheltering. Gardeners in Zone 6 can grow most roses in the tender classes (Chinas, teas, and Noisettes) only with winter protection, although a few are hardy there.

If you want to minimize your labor and losses, marginally hardy plants in some classes can be grown on their own roots. That way, even if the plants are killed to the ground, new growth can spring up from the roots. Indeed, some northern gardeners distinguish between hardy roses and what they call "dieback hardy" varieties: those whose canes may be killed down to the protective snow line but that survive underground and in spring grow rapidly enough to bloom well.

The amount of coverage needed also depends on the roses' site. Plants sheltered by fences or shrubs or sited near the house will endure less damage from winter winds. On the other hand, roses planted in low spots are at greater risk because cold air will pool there.

If your bushes' canes will be partly or completely exposed during winter, consider applying an antitranspirant—a product that coats the plant and reduces moisture loss due to drying winds. Several brands are available in garden centers.

Finally, healthy roses are much more likely to pull through severe winters than plants that have been stressed by disease, drought, or nutrient deficiencies. If plants have had problems with disease, apply a dormant spray (see part

5 for details) before proceeding with winter protection. The spray will kill at least some of the fungus spores on the plant and also the eggs of aphids and spider mites.

Many gardeners choose to defoliate their roses each winter, for two reasons: removing the leaves encourages plants to go dormant and also eliminates fungus spores that would otherwise overwinter on leaves, whether they stay on the bush or fall to the ground. The drawback is that defoliation takes a lot of time and isn't practical for those who have many roses. If you decide to try it, wait until after the first hard freeze.

Following are popular cold-defying techniques, from minimal to extensive, for all roses, with specific instructions for climbing and standard, or tree-form, roses (those grafted to a slender, 2- to 3-foot treelike stem). If you're not sure what's necessary, check with experts in your local rose society.

Mounds and Collars

MOUND AND COLLAR

If your roses require only minimal safeguarding, a mound of dry garden soil or compost around the base of each plant may be all it takes. Apply the mound after the ground freezes, to a height of about 12 inches (6–8 inches for miniatures). As the ground thaws in spring, carefully and gradually remove the mound with a gentle stream from the hose.

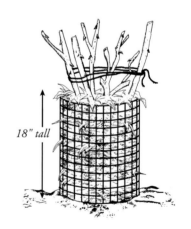

18" tall

For greater protection, tie the canes together with twine before applying the mound. Then build a "collar" around the bush: an 18-inch-high circle of chicken wire or hardware cloth that will keep the mound in place. Once the mound has frozen, cover the canes with evergreen boughs, clean straw, or salt hay to provide further insulation.

If a number of roses are growing close together, build a mega-collar around each cluster of bushes, and after applying individual soil mounds, fill the entire large collar with straw or salt hay.

Complete Coverage

In more severe climates gardeners protect the entire plant, not just the base. Several methods are popular. You can begin with the mound-and-collar technique described above. Cut the canes back so that they're not exposed to the cold and wind, and tie them together with twine. Then wrap the sides and top of the collar (or just the top) with burlap, tied securely in place with twine.

Or cut canes back low enough to fit the plant under a bushel basket. Remove the bottom from the basket; mound dry bark, soil, or peat moss around the crown; put the upside-down basket over the plant; add more mounding material to fill the basket; and cover the whole thing (or just the top) with burlap, secured with twine.

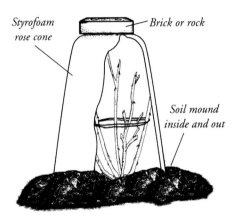

Some growers prefer to use commercial rose cones instead. These Styrofoam shelters do an excellent job of insulating. The basic procedure is the same: cut the canes, tie them together, mound soil or bark around the crown, and put the cone in place, mounding a little more soil around its base. Each cone should have ventilation holes that you can cover with burlap during extremely cold weather. You'll want to weight cones with bricks as well to prevent them from sailing away in a brisk wind.

Styrofoam rose cones offer excellent insulation from cold and protection from wind. A mound of soil around the plant's crown is an additional safeguard.

Ultimate Protection

In the 1950s a clever Minnesota gardener named Albert Nelson developed a method called the Minnesota tip that permits gardeners in the coldest climates to grow hybrid teas and other relatively tender roses. It's a lot of work, but if you live in a severe-winter climate and want to grow a nonhardy rose, give it a try. The first step is to dig up the roots on one side of the plant.

That's so you can bend the plant horizontally (toward the undisturbed roots) and bury it. Now dig a trench to accommodate the canes once the plant has been tipped over. Bend the plant into the trench, and cover everything, from roots to cane tips, with soil.

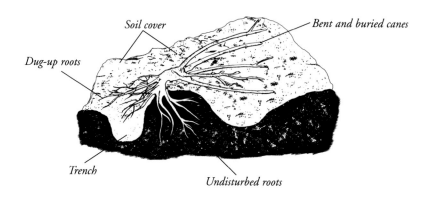

Soil cover

Bent and buried canes

Dug-up roots

Trench

Undisturbed roots

Protecting Standard Roses

Because their bud grafts are exposed to the elements, not safely planted underground, standard roses are especially vulnerable to cold. If you garden in a climate colder than Zone 6 or 7, consider growing your standards in pots. When winter comes and they go dormant, shelter them in an unheated garage, basement, or shed.

If this isn't an option or you'd rather plant your standards in the garden, try one of the following techniques. You can provide moderate protection by gently packing the top of the plant with straw or salt hay, then wrapping the plant—trunk and canes—with burlap. Make sure the bud union and canes are well padded with plant matter. Use twine to hold the burlap securely in place.

In colder regions, protect standards with the Minnesota tip method described above. Leave the plant's support stake in position, and once you've bent the plant over, use two crossed wooden stakes to hold the trunk down before applying the soil cover.

If you don't have room in your flower bed to bend over and trench a good-size standard, consider digging up the entire plant and burying it in the compost pile till spring.

Shielding Climbers and Ramblers

Most climbing and rambling roses—with a few exceptions (for example, Explorer series roses that can be grown as climbers, such as 'John Cabot' and 'William Baffin', hardy to Zone 3)—would endure severe, if not fatal, dieback if unprotected in cold climates. In the coldest regions canes should be removed from their supports and bent to the ground, where they can be held in place with crossed stakes and buried beneath 3 to 4 inches of soil.

The alternative is to remove the canes from their fence or trellis and to tie them to a pole. They can then be insulated with straw or evergreen branches and covered in burlap, held in place with twine.

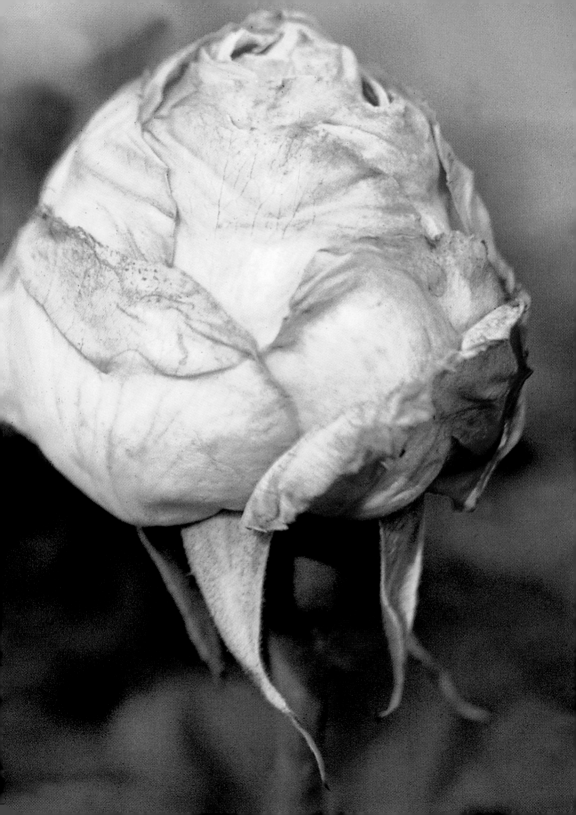

fighting fungi, battling bugs

The Essentials

- The Ever-Present Fungi
- Bacteria and Viruses
- Insects Among Us

125

If you quickly scanned through this section and counted all the things that could possibly plague a rosebush, you might be tempted to devote your efforts to coneflowers or daffodils instead. Fortunately, no rose garden is liable to be troubled by all of the funguses, insects, and other maladies presented here.

And there's a lot you can do to prevent problems or reduce their severity: Plant your roses in the right place (see part 1) and in good soil (see part 2), and make sure they get no more or less water and fertilizer than they really need (see part 4). Choose cultivars with good disease-resistance (see part 3), and don't plant a rose that's showing obvious signs of infection. Remove and throw away diseased or infested leaves and flowers as you notice them; keep the garden clean by getting rid of fallen rose leaves, where bugs and fungi can overwinter, and pruning away diseased wood (see part 4).

These are some of the basic principles of integrated pest management (IPM), an approach that combines cultural, biological, and chemical controls in order to minimize the use of pesticides. IPM practitioners use pesticides only when an infestation has reached a specific threshold and other methods fail to solve the problem. It's a wise philosophy for every gardener. In fact, the Environmental Protection Agency now recommends using pesticides minimally and only after less-toxic approaches have proven ineffective.

Keep in mind that the goal for your rose bed needn't be perfection, presuming you're growing roses for pleasure rather than to exhibit them in shows. It isn't essential that your plants be flawless, just healthy. So if they lose some leaves because of blackspot or are chewed on by Japanese beetles, it isn't the end of the world. You'll enjoy your roses a great deal more—and spend less time fussing with them—if you can accept a certain quota of bugs and fungi as inevitable. If some plants can't survive this laid-back approach, it's your decision: dig them out and make room for tougher roses, or spend the extra time giving them the pampering they need.

You have several options when it comes to dealing with pests. You can do nothing and hope the roses make it. That's certainly the least time-consuming strategy, but you'll probably lose plants that aren't particularly disease- or insect-resistant, and the sicker roses may spread their maladies to healthier specimens.

You can attempt to solve problems as they occur, with a range of products and strategies.

Or you can use pesticides preventively, before you see any evidence of trouble.

The third approach is wise where fungal diseases are concerned because they're easier to prevent than to cure. In fact, gardeners in especially challenging climates, where fungal diseases are rampant, may not have a choice unless all of their roses are ironclad cultivars and species. If you'd prefer not to use traditional fungicides, you'll be glad to know that a few less-toxic formulas are available.

Spraying insecticides preventively, however, isn't recommended in most cases because they end up killing beneficial insects too—those that prey upon harmful bugs and keep pest populations in balance. Some insecticides can harm bees and birds and if used improperly can taint the water supply. Many are also highly toxic to humans.

One good rule of thumb is not to worry about insect pests until you see them or signs of their presence and it appears that predatory insects aren't going to solve the problem. Then take appropriate measures to get rid of them, starting with nontoxic and less-toxic approaches. See the second half of part 5 for specific recommendations.

The Ever-Present Fungi

Fungal diseases are the Achilles' heel of the genus *Rosa*, which includes all the plants we call roses, from single-flowered species to glamorous hybrid teas. Nonetheless, some kinds of roses are more disease-resistant than others. For example, rugosa roses—originally from Korea, Japan, and China—and their hybrids are extremely resistant to both blackspot and powdery mildew, although in certain areas some may be prone to rust.

That illustrates an important point: Each fungal disease needs certain environmental conditions in order to grow and spread. Your climate—temperature range, amount of rainfall, level of humidity—will determine whether blackspot, powdery mildew, rust, and downy mildew will thrive in your area.

This section of the book will give you a good idea what to expect, but it makes sense to get additional information from members of your local rose society or consulting rosarians. They can tell you which diseases are particularly troublesome in your area, which rose varieties among the kinds you like have shown the greatest resistance, and what cultural and treatment strategies are most successful.

Don't let the prevalence of funguses discourage you from growing roses. Some roses will thrive even without sprays. For those that require protection, spraying is a quick and easy job. Dozens of plants can be covered in twenty to thirty minutes every week or two.

DISEASE RESISTANCE AND SUSCEPTIBILITY

The ancestry of most hybrid roses is wide-ranging, so even though certain classes tend to be disease-prone or -resistant, individual members may vary greatly, depending on their genetic background. It's possible to make some generalizations, though.

Most roses are prone to blackspot except in dry areas. Among modern roses, floribundas often have greater disease-resistance than hybrid teas and grandifloras. Old roses are far from immune: more-susceptible classes include hybrid perpetuals, teas, Bourbons, and centifolias.

The majority of fragrant roses are somewhat prone to powdery mildew. Many Bourbons, centifolias, gallicas, mosses, and modern roses are susceptible.

Rugosas and their hybrids, albas, hybrid musks, and roses with wichuraiana ancestors are often resistant to blackspot and powdery mildew; spinosissimas and hybrid multifloras usually have better-than-average blackspot resistance.

Given the right climate, most roses are somewhat susceptible to rust. And it appears that most cultivated varieties can get downy mildew, although response to the disease varies.

Many, but not all, species roses are disease-resistant. It all depends on where they evolved and what they developed defenses against. Species native to your region will be resistant to the prevailing insect and disease problems.

Blackspot

This troublesome fungus is prevalent worldwide except in areas where there's little or no rainfall during the growing season. By the time you see evidence of blackspot, the disease is already established. The most obvious sign—as its name suggests—is round black spots with irregular edges on foliage, and each spot produces new spores that can spread the disease. Yellow patches appear later around the spots, and affected leaves usually die. Young leaves are more vulnerable than older ones. The disease also causes raised, irregular purplish-red blotches to appear on new rose canes. As canes age, these affected areas become blackened and blistered. Blackspot overwinters on fallen leaves and cane lesions.

Rose with blackspot.

Although blackspot makes your roses look ugly, the real damage is caused by defoliation. The consequences are a loss of vigor, reduced ability to survive during winter, and decreased flowering, with lower-quality blooms.

The spores are spread in water droplets, and infection follows if the temperature and moisture level are right. The disease can't develop unless spores stay wet for at least seven hours—the reason gardeners in moist regions are advised not to wet leaves when watering and never to water at night, when leaves would likely stay wet till morning. The optimum temperature for development of the disease is 75°F, and infection is more likely during periods of frequent rainfall and in wet climates.

Powdery Mildew

True to its name, this fungus covers leaves with a powdery whitish or grayish fuzz—looking, in advanced stages, as though someone had poured flour over

Rose with powdery mildew.

affected bushes. It's more subtle when the infection is new, causing slightly raised, blisterlike areas to appear on leaves. As the disease progresses, young leaves may become twisted or rippled; mature leaves are less likely to be infected. The fungus may also grow on young stems and on flower buds. Whereas blackspot is usually most severe on the bottom half of the plant, powdery mildew appears at the top.

The disease reduces the leaves' ability to grow and take in sunlight for photosynthesis, weakening the plant. It overwinters within infected bud eyes and on fallen leaves.

Unlike blackspot, powdery mildew is discouraged by the presence of water on leaves, and spores are spread by wind, not water. For these reasons, some rosarians in mildew-prone regions use jets of water to wet leaves and dislodge fungus spores that haven't yet taken hold. This disease thrives throughout North America but is especially common in drier climates. Development is optimum when days are dry (40 percent to 70 percent relative humidity) and warm (80°F) and nights are humid and cool (60°F). Planting in full sun discourages powdery mildew, as the spores are sensitive to direct sunlight.

Rust

This disease typically affects only roses grown in the Pacific Northwest and other western regions that have mild winters and cool, moist weather during the growing season. In the early stages of a rust infection you'll

Rose with rust.

notice powdery bright-orange pustules on the undersides of the leaves. Later the upper sides of the leaves may show orange or brown spots, and young canes sometimes become distorted. Susceptible plants will eventually defoliate if rust isn't checked.

Like those of blackspot, rust spores need continuous moisture before infection occurs, but only for two to four hours. The optimum temperature for rust development is 64 to 70°F. Summer heat discourages this disease.

Downy Mildew

Fortunately, this potentially devastating disease is less prevalent than blackspot and powdery mildew. It's more likely to appear in the cool, moist climates of the eastern and northern United States, although outbreaks have affected gardens in the South and on the West Coast as well. Young leaves, usually near the top of the bush, develop irregular brown, black, or purplish-red patches, and leaflets usually turn yellow. Grayish fuzz can be seen on the undersides of leaves before color changes occur on top. Small purplish blotches may appear on canes. Defoliation may be dramatically rapid and widespread.

Rose with downy mildew.

There's no danger of downy mildew infection unless the humidity is 85 percent or greater. The best temperature for germination of the disease spores is 65°F; spores are killed if the temperature stays at 80°F for more than twenty-four hours. Hot weather—daily temperatures of 80°F with nighttime lows of 60°F or more—keeps downy mildew in check.

The spores germinate within four hours if leaves are wet or heavy fog is present, and spores are spread in splashing water. If downy mildew is a problem in your area, do your best to keep leaves dry and maximize air circulation.

Other Fungal Diseases

Roses are prey to a few other fungal diseases too, although they're usually less damaging than those described above.

Anthracnose

Occasionally confused with blackspot, anthracnose also causes dark, circular spots to appear on leaves, sometimes with yellow discoloration in surround-

ing areas. The spots may be brown, red, or purplish, and eventually their centers turn whitish, with red margins. The centers may drop out or become thin and papery. Anthracnose spores are dispersed in water, and the disease needs wet conditions in order to take hold. It's more common among cultivars with *Rosa multiflora* or *R. wichuraiana* in their ancestry—a group that includes a number of climbers, ramblers, and polyanthas.

Rose with anthracnose.

Botrytis

A fuzzy grayish-brown mold, botrytis may be seen on buds, flowers, and canes or on bare-root roses. Infected blooms won't open and should be removed and thrown away. Wet, cool conditions encourage botrytis—yet another reason to make sure your roses get morning sun to dry the dew.

Canker

This fungus gains entry when rose canes are wounded during pruning, planting, or cultivation or when they rub against each other. Cankers, as these areas of cane dieback are called, begin as small yellow or reddish spots. Over time the spots

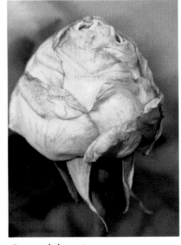

Rose with botrytis.

turn brown and grow larger, while the tissue inside shrinks and dries. Cankers sometimes encircle a cane, killing its top growth. Any damaged rose can be bothered by canker.

Using Fungicides

The fungal diseases described above are usually easy to prevent by spraying an appropriate fungicide every seven to fourteen days. Most rosarians who spray begin their program as soon as leaves begin to appear. If you wait to see the signs of fungal diseases, they already have a foothold.

Some rose growers begin even before the season starts, by applying a dormant spray—made from a lime-sulfur mixture or a heavy horticultural oil that can be used only when plants are leafless—to kill exterior fungus spores overwintering on canes as well as the eggs of aphids and mites.

On the other hand, if you're not sure whether you'll need to spray certain roses, there's no way to find out except to wait and see. In any case, rugosa species and their hybrids should not be sprayed; their leaves react badly to most chemicals.

In order to keep hybrid teas, grandifloras, floribundas, miniatures, Bourbons, and hybrid perpetuals looking decent, most rosarians choose to spray. Others—especially those in less-challenging climates—are able to avoid spraying and are willing to tolerate somewhat higher levels of disease. Best candidates for spray-free gardens include rugosas, albas, the more disease-resistant gallicas and damasks, hybrid musks, some modern shrubs, some polyanthas, and certain species.

Presuming you have the right equipment (see the sidebar on page 135), spraying is simple and takes little time. It is important, though, to read product labels carefully and to observe the instructions and safety precautions. The toxicity of fungicides varies widely, and their labels reflect that. Each commercial product bears signal words that indicate how toxic it is, in categories determined by the Environmental Protection Agency: "danger," highly toxic; "warning," moderately toxic; and "caution," mildly toxic. Because fungi can develop a resistance to overused fungicides, it's wise to alternate between two or three different products.

Following is a list of some of the more popular commercial fungicides and the rose diseases they're most effective against.

Aliette (active ingredient fosetyl-al, signal word "caution"): downy mildew

Benlate, Green Light Systemic Fungicide with Benomyl (active ingredient benomyl, signal word "caution"): powdery mildew, blackspot, rust, anthracnose, botrytis

Bravo, Daconil 2728 (active ingredient chlorothalonil, signal word "warning"): powdery mildew, blackspot, rust, botrytis, anthracnose

Dithane, Maneb, Manzate, Penncozeb (active ingredient mancozeb, signal word "caution"): downy mildew, blackspot

Funginex (active ingredient triforine, signal word "danger"): blackspot, powdery mildew, rust, anthracnose

Green Light Rose Defense (active ingredient extract of neem oil, signal word "caution"): blackspot, powdery mildew, rust, botrytis, anthracnose

Kocide, Mankocide (active ingredient copper hydroxide, signal word "danger," "caution," or "warning," depending on the formulation): downy mildew

Ridomil, Subdue (active ingredient metalaxyl, signal word "warning"): downy mildew

Rubigan (active ingredient fenarimol, signal word "warning" or "caution," depending on the formulation): powdery mildew

Less-toxic Sprays

If you'd like to try a less-toxic fungicide, here are three options. Don't apply when the temperature is above 90°F, as they may burn leaves.

The Bicarbonate Formula

Research at Cornell University in the 1980s proved the effectiveness of sodium bicarbonate—ordinary baking soda—and potassium bicarbonate in combating powdery mildew and, to a lesser degree, blackspot on hybrid teas. The Cornell formula is 3 teaspoons bicarbonate and $2^1/_2$ tablespoons light horticultural spray oil (for example, Sunspray Ultrafine Horticultural Spray Oil) per gallon of water.

Compression sprayer   Unless your rose garden is extensive, a plastic 2- to 3-gallon compression sprayer is usually the best choice; each gallon of spray will cover approximately two dozen roses. Those with hundreds of plants prefer powered sprayers that don't need pumping and dispense a fine mist that makes covering a large number of roses comparatively quick and easy.

Always wear gloves, goggles, long sleeves and pants, and shoes and socks when you spray. Choose a time—preferably early in the morning—when there's little or no wind and when people, animals, birds, and bees aren't active in the area. Never spray during the hottest part of the day or when the temperature exceeds 90°F; if you do, rose leaves may be burned by the spray. Many rosarians also advise watering roses before you spray in order to minimize the danger of spray burn.

Fill the sprayer with water and a proper dose of fungicide, following package directions to the letter, then pump to create the necessary pressure. Begin by spraying the undersides of leaves, then the tops, until the leaves are wet and the spray begins to drip off.

Make only as much spray as you'll need that day; using old spray solution isn't recommended, and the excess can't be dumped into sewers or disposed of in any way that could poison the water supply. If you end up with extra spray, apply it to other ornamentals in the garden, presuming the label indicates the product can safely be used on them. When you're done, wash your clothes.

To keep your sprayer clog-free, rinse it with water after every use; once a month or so run a weak solution of vinegar through it, followed by a water rinse.

Hose-end water wand for spraying soft-bodied insects and spider mites from plants. Good brands include Water Wand for Spider Mites and the Jet-All Water Wand.

Glass or plastic measuring cups and plastic measuring spoons solely for use with pesticides

Sturdy rubber gloves

Goggles or other eye protection

Whole-neem Oil

Made from the neem tree native to India and Burma, neem oil—not to be confused with neem extract, an insecticide—coats leaf surfaces and slows or prevents the germination and adherence of fungus spores. It also appears to help stop existing fungal infections from progressing. Green Light Rose Defense, a neem-oil product labeled for use in preventing powdery mildew, blackspot, rust, anthracnose, and botrytis, also has miticidal (antimite) and insecticidal properties.

Antitranspirants

Antitranspirants are products that coat plants with nontoxic waxes and polymers to slow down the rate at which they transpire, or lose moisture to the air. They're used to help reduce drying due to winter winds, to keep needles on Christmas trees longer, to reduce transplant shock, and most recently to protect leaves from fungal diseases.

Antitranspirants aren't labeled as fungicides, meaning their manufacturers haven't registered them as fungicides and don't claim they are effective as such. But there's no harm in using them according to package directions and achieving fungus protection at the same time. Presumably antitranspirants work by making it harder for fungal spores to penetrate and infect leaves.

Research at Louisiana State University and elsewhere has shown potentially promising results. In blackspot-prone Louisiana, hybrid teas and grandifloras sprayed with any of several commercial antitranspirants every fourteen days showed less than 10 percent defoliation from blackspot, although the products were not as effective during periods of extremely heavy rainfall. Other research indicates that antitranspirants may be effective against powdery mildew too. Treatment must be repeated as new leaves appear and expand. Brand names include Wilt Pruf, Cloud Cover, Folicote, Vapor Gard, and Nu-Film 17.

Bacteria and Viruses

The primary bacterial disease of roses is crown gall, which gets its start when roses are damaged by pruning, improper grafting, "heaving" due to cycles of freezing and thawing during winter, insects, or cultivation. Galls—areas of excessive tissue growth—begin as soft, small, rounded swellings with an irregular surface and a green or whitish color. They usually appear at or below the soil, at the bud union, but galls may also affect canes and roots. Over time they grow darker and become woody. When you spot galls, prune them off. Some experts recommend sterilizing your pruning tools in a solution of one part household bleach to nine parts water to avoid spreading the bacterium. If you're shipped or sold a rose with galls on the roots or crown, ask for a healthy replacement plant. There's no need to eliminate an established plant unless it dies.

Rose with crown gall.

Although a number of viruses may affect roses, the diseases they cause aren't nearly as well understood as fungal maladies. The most significant is rose mosaic—actually caused by several viruses—spread when infected bud wood is grafted to healthy rootstock or clean bud wood to diseased rootstock. Cuttings taken from infected plants will also bear the disease. It's impossible to say how widespread mosaic is since many affected roses show no symptoms. Outward signs—the most common are artistic-looking yellow streaks, rings, and mottling on leaves as well as bright orange or yellow leaf veins—may appear sud-

Rose with mosaic.

denly, although the plant has had the disease since it was propagated.

There's no treatment, but the virus doesn't spread from plant to plant in the garden, so if you have an infected rose, you may as well let it live unless its looks bother you or you'd rather make room for a healthier specimen. It's believed that mosaic reduces plant vigor, flowering, and winter hardiness, so avoid buying virus-infected plants. Some rose nurseries use virus-free bud wood and rootstocks; others aren't so careful. Ask before you buy.

Insects Among Us

It's important to realize that insects aren't the enemy: of the thousands of species in existence, only a small minority are harmful rather than helpful to man. Even those we consider pests have their part to play—at the very least as food for wildlife and other insects. So when you see bugs on your roses and other garden plants, find out what they are before deciding whether they're friends or foes. And try nontoxic and less-toxic controls before bringing out the big guns. As mentioned above, insecticides can do more harm than good by indiscriminately killing beneficial species, ultimately resulting in an increased pest population.

Insects can also become resistant to overused pesticides, as individuals that aren't killed reproduce, creating more chemical-tolerant populations. Finally, don't use a bug-zapper in hopes of reducing the number of pests that prey on roses and people. Research indicates that zappers kill primarily beneficial insects such as honeybees, lacewings, and ladybugs.

The following are common rose pests. It's highly unlikely you'll meet all of them, and you may decide that you can put up with a certain amount of insect damage. The beneficial insects, biological controls, and pesticides mentioned as possible solutions can be purchased through mail-order suppliers and garden centers.

Aphids

The appearance of these small sucking insects is a sure sign that spring is on the way. Some aphid species are lime green; others are black, yellow, or even pink-tinged. Whatever their color, aphids gather around tender new foliage, buds, and canes. Overfertilized roses that produce lots of soft, sappy growth make a tasty dish for them. Aphids produce a sweet substance called honeydew, which appeals to ants and on which a fungus called sooty mold sometimes grows.

Small colonies of aphids don't do a great deal of damage, but in cool weather they multiply rapidly into large colonies. Once that happens, canes may begin to wilt, and buds may be damaged or fail to open.

Aphids are easily knocked off with a jet from a water wand (see the sidebar on page 135). Natural predators include ladybugs and their larvae as well as lacewings, orius bugs, and parasitic wasps. If the popula-

Rose with aphids.

tion gets out of control, try a low-toxicity insecticidal soap, a horticultural oil, or BioNeem, Margosan-O, or Azatin EC (low-toxicity pesticides based on azadirachtin, derived from neem extract). Avoid spraying beneficial insects such as ladybugs and bees.

Cane Borers

Several different species of these tiny wasplike creatures bore into cut canes, where they lay their eggs. If borers are a pest in your area, seal canes with a few drops of white glue or carpenter's glue after pruning. At pruning time, cut away any wood with telltale holes, down to healthy pith.

Rose cane showing borer entry hole.

Japanese Beetles

With their shiny, metallic green plating, Japanese beetles are beautiful insects, now found in all states east of the Mississippi. What they do to roses is anything but attractive, however. These pests burrow into flowers, chewing them and rose leaves into oblivion. After mating, beetles lay their eggs in the soil,

Japanese beetle consuming a rose.

usually under grass roots, where the grubs develop and feed, emerging the next year as adults.

Less-toxic controls include hand-picking and treatment with milky spore disease (the bacterium *Bacillus popilliae*), which kills Japanese beetle grubs and certain other scarab grubs living in the lawn. Milky spore can be very effective and is harmless to beneficial insects, humans, and pets. Its only drawback is the time needed for it to spread throughout the grub population—usually one to three years. For best results in eliminating Japanese beetles, apply milky spore every year or two.

The best time to hand-pick is early morning, when the doomed beetles are sleepy and less active. Simply pluck them from the flower, and dump them into a bucket of soapy water, where they'll drown.

Neem extract shows promise as a Japanese beetle repellent (most pesticides kill beetles only on contact), although treatment is somewhat expensive and should be applied before adult pests appear.

Although beetle traps are widely marketed to homeowners, research indicates that they attract more beetles to the garden than they trap.

Japanese beetles and other pests—including rose chafers, hoplia beetles, cucumber beetles, and May and June beetles—can also be controlled with beneficial nematodes, microscopic roundworms that enter and poison the larvae. Treatment should be carried out in fall or mid- to late spring, before the grubs emerge. Beneficial nematodes are harmless to earthworms, animals, plants, and insects other than those they parasitize.

A number of common contact insecticides may be used, although effectiveness varies, as the beetles themselves must be sprayed.

Midges

Now found in many states, midges have the nasty habit of laying eggs in new growth and in flower buds, which are destroyed when the larvae hatch and feed. The earliest sign of midge infestation is usually small areas of crisp, burned-looking foliage at the tips of new rose growth. Infected canes won't produce blooms and are called blind shoots (although midges are not the only cause of blind shoots). Remove and destroy affected foliage. You may also see tiny flying insects no more than one-twentieth of an inch long near the damaged foliage.

There's not a lot gardeners can do to prevent midge infestation. Once it occurs, the usual prescription for eradicating midges is to apply the pesticide diazinon to the ground, where midge pupae can be found, and to use it or a systemic insecticide such as Orthene as a spray on foliage several times during the growing season. Although extremely effective chemicals, diazinon and Orthene are toxic to bees and other helpful insects. The beneficial insect aphidoletes, or predatory gall midge, preys on the damaging kind.

Rose Slugs

These leaf-eating pests aren't actually slugs, nor are they slimy. The larvae of sawflies, they resemble caterpillars and can be found chewing holes on the upper and lower sides of rose leaves. When you see rose slugs, remove them along with the leaves they're eating. To control severe infestations, apply insecticidal soap. If that fails, try a contact or systemic insecticide labeled for use on roses.

Because rose slugs aren't really caterpillars, Dipel and other products containing *Bacillus thuringiensis* (Bt) will not harm them, although the bacterium will control true caterpillars such as fruit-tree leaf rollers and tobacco budworms (as will azadirachtin-based insecticides). Bt should not be used indiscriminately, as it will also kill larval butterflies and moths.

Rose slugs on foliage.

The beneficial insects known as syrphid flies prey on larval sawflies.

Scale

Scale insects look like tiny shells attached to your rose canes or leaves. The insects inside the shells insert their mouth parts into the plant and suck its juices, reducing the rose's vigor. Adult scales can't flee—they have no legs or wings—but their shells are hard to penetrate. Juvenile "crawlers" are much more vulnerable.

Lacewings, ladybug larvae, orius bugs, and predatory midges and mites prey on immature scale; parasitic wasps feed on adult scale. Horticultural oils and insecticidal soaps are effective at killing crawlers; other pesticides can also be used.

Spider Mites

Especially problematic when the weather is hot and dry, tiny juice-sucking spider mites gather on the undersides of rose leaves, laying their eggs and creating fine webs. If the infestation is severe, affected leaves eventually turn yellow and brown, then fall off.

When you detect mites, blast the pests away every four to five days with a water wand, which research shows can significantly reduce the population. If that doesn't take care of the problem, try a horticultural oil or insecticidal soap. Predator insects include lacewings, orius bugs, other mite species, and ladybugs. Severe infestations can be wiped out with Avid (a miticide made from abamectin, a soil-borne fungus) and a number of contact insecticides.

Spider mite damage.

Thrips

Suspect thrips when you see small brown spots appear on blooms that may fail to open or brown edges on petals. Slender brown, golden, or nearly black insects no more than one-sixteenth of an inch long, thrips prefer light-colored flowers. Adult thrips lay their eggs inside flower buds, which can make it hard to eradicate them. Once the eggs hatch, the tiny worms enter the soil, from which adult thrips shortly emerge. To help reduce the population, remove any infested flowers, and dispose of them in a tightly sealed trash bag.

Rose with thrips.

Thrips have natural enemies, among them a parasitic wasp, a predatory thrips (the word *thrips* is both singular and plural), predatory mites, ladybugs, lacewings, and orius bugs. Insecticidal soap, azadirachtin-based insecticides, and systemic insecticides such as Orthene can be useful.

Inviting Beneficial Insects to Your Garden

You can buy beneficial insects and release them in your garden, but a better—and cheaper—strategy would be to encourage them to show up on their own. If you hope to shelter beneficials, you will need to avoid the use of insecticides or to confine your choices to the least-toxic ones: insecticidal soap, horticultural spray oil, neem extract, and biological controls such as *Bacillus thuringiensis* (Bt) and *B. popilliae* (milky spore).

The ladybug, a beneficial garden resident.

You can also put out a welcome mat by planting herbs, ornamentals, and vegetables that appeal to beneficials—typically small insects that take nectar and pollen from small, shallow blooms in the sunflower, carrot, cabbage, and scabiosa families.

Your garden will be more enticing to beneficial insects if it includes a diversity of flowering plants and a source of water, which could be as simple as a shallow pan at ground level that's refilled every day or two.

If you purchase beneficial insects to correct specific pest problems in the garden, buy from a company whose salespeople can give you detailed information about appropriate species and the correct time to release them. Beneficials are usually most effective in the early stages of an infestation, presuming there's enough food present to keep them around. For more information, see the books and vendors listed in the appendix.

Fall-blooming goldenrod 'Golden Fleece' (Solidago sphacelata, foreground) and New England aster 'Purple Dome' (Aster novae-angliae, left) will both attract helpful insects.

PLANTS THAT ENCHANT BENEFICIALS

The following plants have been determined to attract a variety of desirable insects.

- Herbs and ornamentals: angelica, anise hyssop, aster, candytuft, caraway, caryopteris, ceanothus, chamomile, chervil, clethra, coneflower, coriander, cosmos, daisy, dill, evening primrose, fennel, feverfew, goldenrod, hyssop, lavender, liatris, lovage, marigold, nasturtium, pansy, parsley, pincushion flower, Queen Anne's lace, scabiosa, sunflower, sweet alyssum, tansy, tithonia, white lace flower, yarrow
- Vegetables: broccoli, cabbage, carrot, mustard, parsnip, radish

Rose Resources

Recommended Books

Austin, David. *Old Roses and English Roses.* Woodbridge, Suffolk, U.K., and Wappingers Falls, N.Y.: Antique Collectors' Club, 1992. A good overview of select heirloom varieties and the hybridizer's thoughts on his English-rose breeding program. Color photographs.

Beales, Peter. *Classic Roses.* New York: Henry Holt & Co., 1997. Thorough and authoritative encyclopedia covering hundreds of rose cultivars, old and new. Particularly useful presentation of rose history and the development of classes. Color photographs.

Dickerson, Brent C. *The Old Rose Advisor.* Portland, Ore.: Timber Press, 1992. Extensive guide to repeat-blooming old roses: damask perpetuals, Chinas, teas, Bourbons, hybrid perpetuals, and Noisettes as well as older polyanthas and hybrid teas. Vintage color illustrations; no photographs.

Dobson, Beverly R., and Peter Schneider, editors. *The Combined Rose List.* Self-published. An annual paperback guide to all the roses available in commerce, with specific catalog sources for each cultivar. If you're looking for hard-to-find roses, *The Combined Rose List* is the best and easiest way to locate them. Available from Peter Schneider, P.O. Box 677, Mantua, OH 44255.

Druitt, Liz, and G. Michael Shoup. *Landscaping With Antique Roses.* Newtown, Conn.: Taunton Press, 1992. Very useful guide to incorporating old roses into the garden. Emphasizes tender classes and is geared toward Southern gardeners. Color photographs.

Druitt, Liz. *The Organic Rose Garden.* Dallas: Taylor Publishing, 1996. Thorough and entertaining guide to growing roses without pesticides. Most useful for Southerners. Color photographs.

Martin, Clair G. *100 English Roses for the American Garden.* New York: Workman Publishing, 1997. An expert assessment of David Austin's roses. Color photographs by Saxon Holt.

McCann, Sean. *Miniature Roses.* London: Cassell, 1991. An introduction to the miniature rose's history and cultivation, with information on exhibition, propagation, and hybridizing. Color photographs.

Moody, Mary, and Peter Harkness, editors. *The Illustrated Encyclopedia of Roses.* Portland, Ore.: Timber Press, 1992. Large and thorough guide to more than 1,000 roses of all classes. Color photographs.

Olkowski, William, Sheila Daar, and Helga Olkowski. *The Gardener's Guide to Common-Sense Pest Control.* Newtown, Conn.: Taunton Press, 1995. Integrated-pest-management strategies for avoiding the use of toxic chemicals in the garden. Black-and-white illustrations.

Osborne, Robert. *Hardy Roses*. Pownal, Vt.: Garden Way Publishing, Storey Communications Inc., 1991. Detailed and useful introduction to roses for cold climates. Emphasis on organic pest and disease control. Color photographs by Beth Powning.

Scanniello, Stephen, and Tania Bayard. *Climbing Roses*. New York: Prentice Hall, 1994. Extensive and expert discussion of all manner of climbing and rambling roses. Color photographs.

Scanniello, Stephen, editor. *Easy-Care Roses*. New York: Brooklyn Botanic Garden, 1995. A collection of articles on low-maintenance roses for all parts of the country, as well as landscaping tips and organic cultural strategies. Color photographs.

Scanniello, Stephen. *A Year of Roses*. New York: Henry Holt & Co., 1997. Excellent, authoritative discussion of every aspect of rose culture. Thorough and fun to read. Highly recommended. No photographs.

Schneider, Peter. *Peter Schneider on Roses*. New York: Macmillan, 1995. Part of the Burpee Expert Gardener Series. Authoritative, opinionated, well-written guide to select cultivars and their garden uses. Color photographs. Highly recommended.

Schneider, Peter, editor. *Taylor's Guide to Roses*, revised edition. New York: Houghton Mifflin, 1995. Authoritative handbook, with color photographs and descriptions of about 400 cultivars as well as succinct cultural and historical information.

Starcher, Allison Mia. *Good Bugs for Your Garden*. Chapel Hill, N.C.: Algonquin Books of Chapel Hill, 1995. Charming and useful guide to beneficial insects, their life cycles, and ways to entice them. Attractive color illustrations by the author.

Thomas, Graham Stuart. *The Graham Stuart Thomas Rose Book*. Portland, Ore.: Sagapress/Timber Press, 1994. Masterly discussion of old as well as modern roses and their history, value, and cultivation. Color photographs and vintage illustrations.

Verrier, Suzanne. *Rosa Gallica*. Deer Park, Wis.: Capability's Books, 1996. Excellent and well-researched exploration of the gallicas and their history. Color photographs by the author.

Verrier, Suzanne. *Rosa Rugosa*. Deer Park, Wis.: Capability's Books, 1991. Valuable guide to this hardy, fragrant, and carefree class—perhaps the best beginners' roses. Color photographs.

Zuzek, Kathy, Marcia Richards, Steve McNamara, and Harold Pellett. *Roses for the North*. St. Paul: Minnesota Agricultural Experiment Station, 1995. Research-based information on various cultivars' hardiness, disease- and insect-resistance, and cultivation. Color photographs. For ordering information, write or call MES Distribution Center, 20 Coffey Hall, 1420 Eckles Avenue, St. Paul, MN 55108-6069, 800-876-8636.

Roses by Mail

THE ANTIQUE ROSE EMPORIUM

Route 5, Box 143
Brenham, TX 77833
800-441-0002
Catalog $5.00

Mostly old roses, grown on their own roots; specializes in tender varieties.

ARENA ROSE COMPANY

P.O. Box 3096
Paso Robles, CA 93447
805-227-4094
Catalog $5.00

Exhibition varieties and English roses.

EDMUNDS' ROSES

6235 S.W. Kahle Road
Wilsonville, OR 97070
888-481-7673
Web site www.edmundsroses.com
Catalog free

Popular exhibition varieties and other modern roses.

HEIRLOOM OLD GARDEN ROSES

24062 N.E. Riverside Drive
St. Paul, OR 97137
503-538-1576
Catalog $5.00

Very large selection of antique roses, the largest English-rose selection of any U.S. catalog retailer, a number of Buck roses, etc. All are own-root.

HORTICO

723 Robson Road, R.R. 1
Waterdown, Ontario LOR 2H1, Canada
905-689-9323
Web site hortico.bigwave.ca
Catalog $3.00 (can be downloaded free on Web site)

Very large selection of roses of all kinds.

JACKSON & PERKINS

P.O. Box 1028
Medford, OR 97501
800-292-4769
Web site www.jackson-perkins.com
Catalog free

Mostly modern varieties, including some English roses, with a few old roses.

JUSTICE MINIATURE ROSES

5947 S.W. Kahle Road
Wilsonville, OR 97070-9727
503-682-2370
Catalog free

Large selection of miniature roses.

SAM KEDEM GREENHOUSE AND NURSERY

12414 191st Street East
Hastings, MN 55033
612-437-7516
Catalog $2.00

Hardy roses of many kinds, including a large selection of Buck varieties.

MICHAEL'S PREMIER ROSES

9759 Elder Creek Road
Sacramento, CA 95829
916-369-7673
Web site www.michaelsrose.com
Catalog free

Many miniatures as well as old and other modern roses.

NOR'EAST MINIATURE ROSES INC.

58 Hammond Street
P.O. Box 307
Rowley, MA 01969
978-948-7964
Web site www.noreast-miniroses.com/index.html
Catalog free

Good selection of miniature roses, particularly those hybridized by Harm Saville.

PETALUMA ROSE COMPANY

P.O. Box 750953

Petaluma, CA 94975

707-769-8862

Web site www.sonic.net/~petrose

Catalog free

Modern varieties, shrubs, old roses, and a large selection of English roses.

REGAN NURSERY

4268 Decoto Road

Fremont, CA 94555

510-797-3222

Web site www.regannursery.com

Catalog $3.00

Extensive selection of old and modern roses of all kinds.

THE ROSERAIE AT BAYFIELDS

P.O. Box R

Waldoboro, ME 04572

207-832-6330

Web site www.roseraie.com

Catalog free

Hardy old and modern roses, including Buck and English varieties.

ROSES UNLIMITED

Route 1, Box 587, N. Deerwood Drive

Laurens, SC 29360

864-682-7673

Catalog free

Own-root roses, including some Buck varieties and hard-to-find AARS winners.

ROYALL RIVER ROSES

P.O. Box 370

Yarmouth, ME 04096

207-829-5830

Catalog $3.00

Hardy roses old and new, most on their own roots.

SEQUOIA NURSERY

MOORE MINIATURE ROSES

2519 E. Noble Avenue

Visalia, CA 93292

209-732-0190

Catalog free

Miniature roses, especially those hybridized by Ralph Moore, and unusual varieties.

SPRING VALLEY ROSES

P.O. Box 7

Spring Valley, WI 54767

715-778-4481

Web site www.springvalleyroses.com

Catalog $1.00

Hardy and old roses grown on their own roots.

TINY PETALS NURSERY

489 Minot Avenue

Chula Vista, CA 91910-4833

619-422-0385

Catalog free

Miniature roses, especially those hybridized by Dee Bennett.

VINTAGE GARDENS

2833 Old Gravenstein Highway South

Sebastopol, CA 95472

707-829-2035

Web site www.vintagegardens.com

Catalog $5.00, availability list free

Catalog is extensive, listing many hard-to-find older varieties.

WAYSIDE GARDENS

1 Garden Lane

Hodges, SC 29695-0001

800-845-1124

Web site www.waysidegardens.com

Catalog free

Modern roses, including shrubs and English roses, as well as heirloom varieties.

WITHERSPOON ROSE CULTURE

P.O. Box 52489

Durham, NC 27717-2489

800-643-0315

Web site netmar.com/~wrc

Catalog free

All-America Rose Selections winners, Weeks Roses, and other modern roses; a few antique varieties.

Garden Supplies and Equipment

ARBICO INC.

Attn: Acosta
5116 Williamsburg Road
Brentwood, TN 37027
615-370-4301
Web site www.usit.net/hp/bionet/generalists.html
Catalog free

Beneficial insects and other nontoxic lawn- and garden-care products.

THE BUG STORE

113 W. Argonne
St. Louis, MO 63122
800-455-2847
Web site www.bugstore.com
Catalog free

Beneficial insects and other nontoxic means of pest control.

DRIPWORKS

231 E. San Francisco Street
Willits, CA 95490
800-616-8321
Web site www.dripworksusa.com
Catalog free

Do-it-yourself drip irrigation and other efficient watering systems.

GARDENER'S SUPPLY COMPANY
128 Intervale Road
Burlington, VT 05401-2850
800-863-1700
Web site www.gardeners.com
Catalog free

Less-toxic fertilizers and pesticides, beneficial insects, and other supplies.

GARDENS ALIVE!
5100 Schenley Place
Lawrenceburg, IN 47025
812-537-8650
Catalog free

Less-toxic garden products, beneficial insects, and other supplies.

A. M. LEONARD INC.
241 Fox Drive
Piqua, OH 45356
800-543-8955
Web site www.amleo.com
Catalog free

Pruning shears, saws, loppers, spades, and other gardening and landscaping tools.

Organizations

THE AMERICAN HORTICULTURAL SOCIETY

7931 E. Boulevard Drive
Alexandria, VA 22308-1300
703-768-5700
Web site www.ahs.org

Annual dues of $45 include 12 issues of *The American Gardener* magazine, book discounts, and other benefits. The AHS's well-designed full-color magazine is authoritative, often presenting information on current horticultural research. Keen gardeners will learn much about all aspects of horticulture and enjoy an occasional rose article.

THE AMERICAN ROSE SOCIETY

P.O. Box 30000
Shreveport, LA 71130-0030
318-938-5402
Web site www.ars.org

The national organization for U.S. rose-lovers and exhibitors. The ARS publishes a monthly full-color magazine, *American Rose*, and the *American Rose Annual* as well as the annual *Handbook for Selecting Roses*. Individual membership is $32 ($30 for those over age 65) and includes a subscription to one's ARS district organization newsletter. Members also receive discounts on books and other benefits. In recent years the ARS has offered much more information of interest to those who grow heritage roses or practice organic rose gardening. The Web site presents numerous articles on all aspects of rose care and exhibition and an extensive series of links. To locate a consulting rosarian (CR) in your area who will answer your rose questions at no charge, call the ARS or visit the Web site. You need not be a member to contact CRs.

THE CANADIAN ROSE SOCIETY

10 Fairfax Crescent
Scarborough, Ontario M1L 1Z8, Canada
416-757-8809
Web site www.mirror.org/groups/crs/

Benefits include *The Rosarian* magazine, published three times a year, and *The Rose Annual* as well as access to expert rosarians who can answer cultural and other questions. Regular individual membership is $21 (Canadian or U.S.). The Web site includes lists of recommended roses for gardeners in various climates, photographs of and information on hardy roses, links to other rose sites, and more.

THE HERITAGE ROSE FOUNDATION

1512 Gorman Street
Raleigh, NC 27606

A nonprofit corporation created to preserve and study old garden roses. Publishes a quarterly newsletter with brief articles on antique roses and other topics of interest. Membership costs $10 per year. For more information, write the address above, enclosing a self-addressed, stamped envelope.

HERITAGE ROSES GROUP

1034 Taylor Avenue
Alameda, CA 94501

Dedicated to the cultivation of old roses, the Heritage Roses Group publishes a quarterly newsletter with short articles on old roses and regional news and events listings. Membership costs $6 per year, and payment is made to one's regional coordinator. Write for more information, enclosing a self-addressed, stamped envelope.

Newsletters and Magazines

THE AMERICAN ROSE

(see the listing for the American Rose Society, above)

AMERICAN ROSE RAMBLER

P.O. Box 677
Mantua, OH 44255
330-296-2618

Bimonthly, $12 annually. Edited by Peter Schneider, this black-and-white newsletter presents book reviews, cultural tips, updates on new rose registrations, and much more authoritative and entertaining information of interest to rose gardeners. Highly recommended.

FINE GARDENING

The Taunton Press Inc.
63 S. Main Street
P.O. Box 5506
Newtown, CT 06470-5506
203-426-8171

Bimonthly, $32 annually. *Fine Gardening* is a how-to magazine par excellence, printed in full color and beautifully designed. Only occasional articles on roses, but each issue's features on various aspects of horticulture and garden design make it an excellent choice for anyone wishing to learn more about ornamentals.

Web Sites

THE AMERICAN ROSE SOCIETY

www.ars.org

Extensive links and numerous articles on rose care.

BUGS AND ROSES HOMEPAGE

www.concentric.net/~bugman

Informative sections on integrated pest management, rose care, and more by environmental research scientist and rosarian Baldo Villegas.

THE ROSE RESOURCE

www.rose.org

Information about AARS winners and rose culture.

SUITE 101 ROSE PAGE

www.suite101.com/topics/page.cfm/513

Excellent series of articles by landscaper and American Rose Society consulting rosarian Mark Whitelaw as well as question-and-answer forum.

SUPPLIERS OF BENEFICIAL ORGANISMS IN NORTH AMERICA

www.cdpr.ca.gov/docs/ipminov/bensuppl.htm

Information on more than 140 commercial sources of beneficial insects; document can be viewed online or downloaded.

YESTERDAY'S ROSE

www.halcyon.com/cirsium/rosegal

S. Andrew Schulman's guide to old and old-fashioned roses, with good links and tips on finding the proper roses for various hardiness zones and garden situations.

USDA Plant Hardiness Zone Map

AVERAGE ANNUAL MINIMUM TEMPERATURE		
Temperature (°C)	Zone	Temperature (°C)
-45.6 and Below	1	Below -50
-42.8 to -45.5	2a	-45 to -50
-40.0 to -42.7	2b	-40 to -45
-37.3 to -40.0	3a	-35 to -40
-34.5 to -37.2	3b	-30 to -35
-31.0 to -34.4	4a	-25 to -30
-28.9 to -31.6	4b	-20 to -25
-26.2 to -28.8	5a	-15 to -20
-23.4 to -26.1	5b	-10 to -15
-20.6 to -23.3	6a	-5 to -10
-17.8 to -20.5	6b	0 to -5
-15.0 to -17.7	7a	5 to 0
-12.3 to -15.0	7b	10 to 5
-9.5 to -12.2	8a	15 to 10
-6.7 to -9.4	8b	20 to 15
-3.9 to -6.6	9a	25 to 20
-1.2 to -3.8	9b	30 to 25
1.6 to -1.1	10a	35 to 30
4.4 to 1.7	10b	40 to 35
4.5 and Above	11	40 and above

The Gardener's Language

For definitions related to flower forms and parts, see page 41.

All-America Rose Selections (AARS)   A nonprofit organization that tests new hybrid teas, grandifloras, floribundas, miniatures, and landscape shrubs and awards the AARS designation to those that have performed well in about two dozen trial gardens throughout the United States. AARS roses are identified with distinctive metal tags; recent winners are widely available in garden centers.

American Rose Society (ARS)   A nonprofit organization of rose gardeners and exhibitors, with headquarters in Shreveport, Louisiana.

Anerkannte Deutsche Rose (ADR) trials   A three-year endurance test for roses conducted in Germany. Winners must thrive without the application of fungicide or insecticide sprays.

Antitranspirant   A product that coats plants with nontoxic waxes or polymers to slow down the rate at which they transpire, or lose moisture to the air. Antitranspirants help reduce drying due to winter winds and prevent transplant shock; they've also been used to protect rose foliage from fungal diseases.

Balanced fertilizer   A product containing the chemicals nitrogen (N), phosphorus (P), and potassium (K), the nutrients plants require in the largest quantities. Product labels use a series of numbers (for example, 10-10-10 or 20-13-10) to indicate the formulation's percentages of N, P, and K, respectively.

Bare-root   A dormant plant that is shipped to the consumer or a nursery with no soil around its roots. Bare-root plants are available only in late winter and early spring.

Basal break   A new rose cane, or main stem, growing from the plant's graft, or bud union.

Bud eyes   Nodes—just above the juncture of leaves and canes—from which new canes may grow, particularly if stimulated by pruning.

Bud union, or graft   In grafted roses, the knobby swelling where a bud eye from a named rose variety was grafted to an understock.

Bud wood   Rose cuttings from which bud eyes for propagation are taken.

Canes   A rose's main stems.

Class   A specific group of roses that share similar growth habits, flower shapes, foliage, and other characteristics. Although more than three dozen classes exist, by the American Rose Society's latest reckoning, the vast majority of new introductions fall into one of five classes: miniature, shrub, floribunda, grandiflora, and hybrid tea.

Code name   In recent years new roses have been assigned codes that identify both the plants and the hybridizers or firms introducing them—for example, 'JACpico' for the Jackson & Perkins rose 'Pristine'; 'HARpade' for 'Escapade', introduced by England's Jack Harkness; and 'SAValife' for 'Rainbow's End', hybridized by Harm Saville of Nor'East Miniature Roses. Code names can be useful when a rose has been given more than one cultivar name: for instance, the rose known in the United States as 'Elina' is sold in England as 'Peaudouce', but both bear the code name 'DICjana'.

Consulting rosarian (CR)   An expert volunteer certified by the American Rose Society and willing to offer free rose-growing information and advice. To locate the nearest CR, call the ARS at 318-938-5402.

Containerized   Roses sold planted in pots, cardboard boxes, or other containers, with soil around their roots.

Cultivar   A cultivated variety—a unique hybridized plant selection (not a species).

Defoliation   The loss of leaves.

Dieback hardy   Term describing roses whose canes may be killed down to the ground or the protective snow line in winter but that will survive underground and in spring grow rapidly enough to bloom well, despite the dieback.

Dormant spray   A pesticide formulation that can be used only when plants are dormant. Such sprays kill exterior fungus spores overwintering on rose canes as well as the eggs of aphids and mites.

Double-digging   An excellent though labor-intensive method of preparing soil for planting. Double-digging involves dividing a garden bed into a series of trenches and loosening and amending the subsoil and topsoil in a two-stage process.

Exhibition variety   A rose with the demonstrated ability to win awards in rose shows. Popular exhibition varieties may also make good garden plants but are prized primarily for their flower form.

Feeder roots   Numerous small roots a plant uses to take up moisture and nutrients.

Fungicide   A pesticide that prevents or inhibits the growth and spread of fungal diseases.

Grade   An indication of a grafted rose's size, maturity, and quality, according to standards set by the American Nursery & Landscape Association. The best—grade roses 1—must be two years old when harvested from the field, have at least three large, healthy canes of a specified thickness, and meet other qualifications.

Grafting   Technique in which a bud eye from a cultivar is joined to a vigorous rootstock, producing plants more cheaply and quickly than can be done through rooting rose cuttings.

Hardy   A relative term indicating a plant's ability to survive cold winter temperatures. Generally speaking, roses that can endure Zone 5 weather without winter protection are considered hardy; those capable of surviving without protection in USDA Zones 3 and 4 are extremely hardy. The important consideration is whether a rose is hardy enough for your climate.

Horticultural oils   Formulations used to help control insects and diseases on roses and other ornamentals. Heavy horticultural oils can be used as pesticide sprays when roses are dormant and leafless; light horticultural spray oils can be used year-round except during the hottest weather. Read and follow label instructions carefully.

Integrated pest management (IPM)   An approach that combines cultural, biological, and chemical methods of disease and insect control in order to minimize the use of pesticides.

Lateral   A side shoot growing from a cane.

Loam   Easy-to-till, well-draining soil made up of 30–50 percent sand, less than 20 percent clay, and 30–50 percent silt.

Minnesota tip   A radical winter-protection technique that permits gardeners in the coldest climates to grow hybrid teas and other relatively tender roses. The gardener must dig up roots on one side of the plant, dig a trench on the opposite side, bend the plant toward the undisturbed roots so the canes can rest in the trench, and cover the entire horizontal plant with soil.

Modern rose   Any variety belonging to a class created after 1867, the somewhat arbitrary date dividing old and modern roses. Modern classes include hybrid tea, polyantha, miniature, and rambler.

Moss   Pine- or resin-scented glandular growth that appears on rosebuds and stems of certain roses. Nearly all mossed varieties fall within the moss class, part of the group of old garden roses; the exceptions are the mossed miniature roses (for example, 'Dresden Doll' and 'Scarlet Moss') bred by modern-day hybridizer Ralph Moore.

Nematodes   Microscopic roundworms that live in soil. Beneficial nematodes are useful organisms that poison Japanese beetles and other pests.

Old garden rose (OGR)   Any rose belonging to a class created before 1867. The large group of old garden roses comprises many classes, among them alba, Ayrshire, Bourbon, China, tea (not to be confused with the hybrid tea class), damask, eglanteria, gallica, hybrid perpetual, and Portland.

Organic fertilizer   Any natural material such as fish emulsion or meal, blood meal, bone meal, alfalfa meal, cottonseed meal, compost, or manure, applied as a source of plant nutrients and as a soil conditioner.

Organic matter   The decaying remains of plants and animals, used to enrich soil and improve its tilth.

Own-root   A rose whose top growth and root system are of the same variety, that is, one propagated from rooting a softwood cutting rather than grafting a bud eye of a specific variety to an understock. The cutting eventually grows into a mature plant.

Pesticide   A formulation used to kill insects, disease organisms, or both.

pH   A measure of a substance's acidity or alkalinity, on a scale from 1 to 14, with numbers below 7 indicating acidity, 7 indicating neutrality, and numbers above 7 indicating alkalinity. The ideal pH for roses is slightly acidic, between 6.0 and 6.5. If soil pH is too high or low, nutrients become less available to plants.

Prickles   Rose thorns.

Prune To cut back rose canes in order to shape the plant, encourage growth and bloom, and control diseases.

Rootstock In a grafted plant, the vigorous, rapidly growing species or variety that supplies the roots but not the top growth. Roses commonly used as rootstocks include the species *Rosa multiflora* and *R. canina* and named varieties 'Dr. Huey', 'Manetti', and, in the Deep South, 'Fortuniana'.

Shrub Four classes of roses—kordesii, hybrid musk, hybrid rugosa, and shrub—make up the shrub group. Shrubs, generally touted as easy-care landscape roses, have enjoyed a great increase in popularity in the last decade.

Signal words On a pesticide label, an indication of the product's toxicity—"danger" (highly toxic), "warning" (moderately toxic), or "caution" (mildly toxic).

Softwood cutting A firm but not woody section of cane cut from the current season's growth and placed in moist soil or sand so that roots will form. The resulting own-root plant is a genetic clone of its parent.

Soil test Analysis of a given soil sample that indicates the pH and the levels of essential plant nutrients such as potassium and phosphorus. Soil-test results typically include fertilization schedules and other recommendations to correct nutrient deficiencies or a pH that is too high or low.

Species rose A "wild," or naturally occurring, rose.

Sport A spontaneous genetic mutation. A branch that sports may have different-colored blooms, the ability to climb, the capacity for repeat-bloom, or other characteristics that distinguish it from the mother plant.

Standard, or tree, rose A rose grafted to a short, treelike stem, usually 2 or 3 feet tall. Not to be confused with roses in the class alba, in ancient times called tree roses because of their tall stature.

Sucker In a grafted rose, a shoot growing from the rootstock rather than from the named variety grafted to it.

Tender A relative term indicating a lack of winter hardiness. Some modern roses (notably, a number of hybrid teas) and certain classes of old garden roses (for example, teas and Noisettes) are generally tender, or unable to survive in Zones 6 and lower without winter protection.

Tilth Soil texture, specifically, how easy or difficult a soil is to dig and how readily roots can grow in it.

Trace minerals Chemicals such as boron, molybdenum, and zinc that roses need only in small amounts. Some balanced fertilizers include trace minerals in addition to nitrogen, phosphorus, and potassium.

USDA hardiness zones Geographic divisions of North America according to average minimum winter temperatures. Plants are said to be hardy to a particular zone or hardy within a specific zone range, meaning that they can survive winters within the designated areas. See the USDA Plant Hardiness Zone Map on page 160.

Vegetative propagation In roses, the process of producing new plants by rooting softwood cuttings.

Index

Page numbers in *italics* indicate photographs or illustrations.